COME, LORD JESUS

COME, LORD JESUS

Biblical Prayers
with Psalms and Scripture Readings

by

Lucien Deiss, C.S.Sp.

7828

WORLD LIBRARY PUBLICATIONS

3815 N. Willow Rd. • Schiller Park, Illinois 60176

NIHIL OBSTAT: Lawrence J. Mick
 Censor Deputatus
IMPRIMATUR: Daniel E. Pilarczyk, V.G.
 Auxiliary Bishop of Cincinnati
February 20, 1981

Translation of several of the prayers following the psalms in Part Two was made by Paul Welch.
Translation of the prayers in Part Four was made under the direction of Fr. Alcuin L. Mikulanis, O.F.M.
Edited by Nancy Simons.
Cover design by Kathryn Gambetta.

A major portion of this work was published in France as *Prières Bibliques en Église,* Editions du Levain, Paris, 1977.

ISBN: 0-937690-18-X
Library of Congress Catalog Card Number: 80-52315

First Printing: 1981
Printed and bound in the United States of America.

ACKNOWLEDGEMENTS

The psalm texts in Part Two, pages 9-84, are taken from *The Psalms: A New Translation,* ©1963 by the Grail, England, published by William Collins Sons & Co., Ltd., Glasgow, and are used by permission. The psalm numbers follow the Hebrew numbering system. American spelling is used in the texts. The italics in Psalms 42, 43, and 67 are the author's.

The canticle texts in Part Two, pages 85-92, and the Old and New Testament texts in Part Three, pages 95-111, are taken from the *New American Bible,* copyright ©1970 by the Confraternity of Christian Doctrine, Washington, D.C., and are used by license of said copyright owner. No part of the *New American Bible* may be reproduced in any form without permission in writing. All rights reserved.

The texts of the Gospel Canticles, pages 112-113, are from the International Consultation on English Texts.

All other texts from Scripture are the author's translations.

For additional copyright notices, see page 325.

CONTENTS

THE PASCHAL CYCLE

PENTECOST AND THE CHURCH

HOLY MARY

PRAYERS FOR ALL SEASONS ▲

FOREWORD

Come, Lord Jesus is an expansion of the book first published as *Biblical Prayers*. This new book contains all the prayers of *Biblical Prayers* and, in addition, a large selection of psalms (pp. 9-84) and readings from Scripture (pp. 95-111), as well as introductory hymns.

We hope this book will render Christian prayer easier by furnishing all the texts necessary for personal or communal prayer.

The use of these prayers, according to the tradition of the Church, is described on pages xii-xvi.

The Spirit of God assures that by our prayers we may hasten the coming of the Day of the Lord (2 Peter 3:12). May these prayers help to hasten the coming of the Day of God's love over us and help us to pray, "Come, Lord Jesus."

— The Editor

This is not a book for "reading," but for "praying." So often we find it difficult to say the name of God and to praise his love! These prayers are meant to help. You will carry the essential burden and, at the same time, experience the most profound joy in using these formulas — they are only crutches! — to walk toward God and to encounter his love.

These prayers have their roots in Scripture. Other formulas, more up-to-date, may be desirable, even necessary. For my part, I have labored too long in the field of Scripture to wish to reap elsewhere with such abundance; I have walked too long in the forest of Tradition to be able to forget the splendors that I have encountered there.

It is precisely the experience of the timeliness of the Word for all ages, of its harmonious adaptability to our wonderful world of today — the most beautiful because it is our own and the only one in which God speaks to us — that I would like to share with you.

Lucien Deiss, C.S.Sp.
December 8

On the Feast of Our Lady,
"Servant of the Word"

HOMILY OF SAINT AUGUSTINE

O FRATRES, O FILII, O CATHOLICA GERMINA,
O SANCTA ET SUPERNA SEMINA,
O IN CHRISTO REGENERATI ET DESUPER NATI,
AUDITE ME, IMMO PER ME:
CANTATE DOMINO CANTICUM NOVUM.
'ECCE' INQUIS 'CANTO.'
CANTAS, PLANE CANTAS, AUDIO.
SED CONTRA LINGUAM TESTIMONIUM NON DICAT VITA.
CANTATE VOCIBUS,
CANTATE CORDIBUS,
CANTATE ORIBUS,
CANTATE MORIBUS:
CANTATE DOMINO CANTICUM NOVUM.
QUAERITIS QUID DECANTETIS DE ILLO QUEM AMATIS?
SINE DUBIO DE ILLO QUEM AMAS CANTARE VIS.
LAUDES EIUS QUAERIS QUAS CANTAS.
AUDISTIS: *CANTATE DOMINO CANTICUM NOVUM.*
LAUDES QUAERITIS?
LAUS EIUS IN ECCLESIA SANCTORUM.
LAUS CANTANDI EST IPSE CANTATOR.
LAUDES VULTIS DICERE DEO?
VOS ESTOTE QUOD DICATIS.
LAUS IPSIUS ESTIS, SI BENE VIVATIS.

SERMO HABITUS CARTHAGINE AD MAIORES
De responsorio Psalmi 149:
CANTATE DOMINO CANTICUM NOVUM, Sermo XXXIV, 6.
Corpus Christianorum, Series Latina, XLI, p. 426.

HOMILY OF SAINT AUGUSTINE
on
SING TO THE LORD A NEW SONG!
Psalm 149

O CHILDREN OF THE CATHOLIC CHURCH!

O HOLY AND HEAVENLY FLOWERS!

O YOU RESTORED IN CHRIST AND BORN AGAIN

FROM ON HIGH:

LISTEN TO ME, OR BETTER STILL,

LISTEN THROUGH ME:

SING TO THE LORD A NEW SONG!

SEE — YOU SAY — I SING!

YOU SING, YOU SING WELL, I HEAR THAT.

BUT MAY YOUR LIVES NOT BEAR WITNESS

AGAINST YOUR SONG!

SING WITH YOUR VOICES!

SING WITH YOUR HEARTS!

SING WITH YOUR LIPS!

SING WITH YOUR LIVES!

SING TO THE LORD A NEW SONG!

DO YOU SEEK HIM WHOSE PRAISE YOU SING?...

DO YOU SEEK HIS PRAISE?

HIS PRAISE IS IN THE GATHERING OF THE HOLY ONES.

THE PRAISE OF THE ONE YOU SING TO

IS THE SINGERS THEMSELVES.

DO YOU WANT TO OFFER PRAISE TO GOD?

BE YOURSELVES WHAT YOU SING!

YOU ARE HIS PRAISE, IF YOU ARE LIVING RIGHTLY!

Homily of St. Augustine on Psalm 149: *Sing to the Lord a New Song,*
in Carthage, in the Basilica Ad Maiores where Saint Perpetua and
Saint Felicity were buried.

INTRODUCTION

Part One
OPENING VERSES AND HYMNS

Beginning Our Prayer   *Pages 2-5*

After the (optional) opening verse, you may

• begin with a blessing;

• sing one of the opening hymns on pages 2-5; *or*

• sing or recite one of the opening psalms: Psalm 24 (p.17), Psalm 67 (p.35), Psalm 95 (p.50), or Psalm 100 (p.53); *or*

• engage in silent, individual prayer before God the Lord.[1]

Part Two
THE PSALMS AND CANTICLES

Praying the Psalms   *Pages 9-92*

You will find the psalms[2] as well as the biblical canticles on pages 9-92.

• Pray the psalms
—with Jesus Christ, to God the Father, *or*
—with the Church, to Christ the Lord.

• Paul tells us we do not know how to pray as we ought, but the Spirit himself, who dwells in us, will come to help us in our weakness. He prays in us according to the mind of the Father (Romans 8:26-27). Thus the Holy Spirit not only inspires us to pray, but also, through the psalms, puts into our hearts the words that are especially acceptable to the Father. As we pray the psalms, we lend Christ our hearts and lips, so that he can, through them and the Holy Spirit, praise and implore the Father for us.

• There is a history of Christ revealed in the psalms (Luke 24:44). It remains for us, then, to discover, in every psalm, the face of Jesus Christ.

Part Three
THE WORD OF GOD

Celebrating the Word of God Pages 95-114

• The most important element in Christian prayer is listening, not speaking, to God, who speaks to us in his Word. The celebration of the Word of God, therefore, is essential in Christian prayer.

• In order to celebrate this Word, we may read a Scripture text
—that is taken from the Mass of the day, *or*
—that we ourselves have chosen from the treasury of the Bible, *or*
—that is offered on pages 95-111.

• A short homily may celebrate the Word the Lord speaks to us.[3]

• After the reading and the homily, keep silence in your hearts. Pray, "Speak, Lord, your servant is listening." Try to discover in your heart and mind how you can respond to the Word of God spoken in your life today.

Part Four
PRAYER

Responding to the Word Pages 118-302

Prayer is response to the Word of God.[4] This response, according to Christian tradition, may proceed as follows:

• praying the *Canticle of Zechariah* (p.113) at morning prayer or the *Canticle of Mary* or *Simeon* (p.112) at evening prayer;

• expressing our intentions of prayer in the form of a *litany*,[5]
—which consists of the statement of intentions followed by a response *and*
—which may conclude with the statement of private intentions;

• a few moments of *silent prayer*, during which we can speak more personally with the Lord, offering him our hearts;

• praying the *Our Father;*

• praying a final *oration;*[6]

• concluding with a *blessing* or *doxology*.[7]

Christian tradition likes to fulfill the prophecy of Mary, "All ages to come shall call me blessed," by singing her praises. In this spirit, one may sing a short song to Mary. See the text of traditional antiphons on page 310.

NOTES
for pages xii and xiii

1. *Time of silence*

It is possible in community prayer to enhance the silence with good organ music or by playing appropriate records or tapes. This is the time when we prepare our bodies to pray in peace and we lift our hearts to the Lord.

2. *Choice of the psalms*

We have not reproduced in this book the 150 psalms that can easily be found in the Bible. Instead, we present a large selection of them that are easy to pray and that enrich our dialogue with God.

All the psalms, because they are inspired by the Holy Spirit, have the immense dignity of the Word of God. Also they give witness to the history of the chosen people. All the psalms, however, do not have the same facility to express Christian prayer. For instance, we no longer pray *against* our enemies, since the Lord has asked us to pray *for* them, and to love them from the depths of our hearts. (These prayers against the enemy belong, however, to the history of Israel, express confidence in the justice of God, and point the way toward the New Testament.) Some psalms also require a knowledge of the history and geography of Israel that the faithful ordinarily would not have the opportunity to acquire.

In some psalms, too, certain verses that are too difficult to integrate into our Christian prayer are omitted. For instance, in Psalm 137, we omit verse 9, "Happy is the man who takes your little ones and smashes them against the rock!" In this case, the omission is indicated by an ellipsis.

The aim of this choice of psalms is not to place a screen between the faithful and the Word, but rather to facilitate immediate access to biblical prayer for all the faithful. The purpose of prayer is not to recite the psalms, but to meet Jesus Christ and to praise the Father with him.

About the number of psalms to be prayed — in former times Lauds and Vespers were comprised of five psalms each, plus the *Benedictus* in the one and the *Magnificat* in the other. The reform of Vatican II reduced their number to three. Let us, therefore, remember the words of the Lord in his Sermon on the Mount, "When you pray, do not use numerous repetitions as the pagans do. They think they will be heard for their much speaking" (Matthew 6:7). One psalm prayed with close attention and at a moderate pace is more effective as a good prayer than numerous psalms prayed in haste.

3. Homily

In a community celebration, a short homily is recommended to express the mystery of the Word of God, as the Lord explained in his homily in Nazareth, "Today this word is fulfilled as you listen to it" (Luke 4:21).

4. Classification of prayers

The prayers in Part Four are classified according to the seasons of the liturgical year: Advent, Christmas and Epiphany, Lent and Passiontide, the Paschal Cycle, Pentecost and the Church, feasts of Our Lady, and finally the largest section, "Prayers for All Seasons."

The boundaries of the seasons are flexible. Thus, an Advent or Lenten prayer may be used anytime during the year. It is for this reason that, at the bottom of some pages, there are notes offering useful suggestions.

In most sections, the litanies precede the orations.

5. Litanies

Intentions

Some litanies propose a large number of intentions. The assembly can thus choose those that are best suited to its prayer. It is always better to surprise the community by moderation rather than excess.

Responses of the assembly

The response is printed at the beginning of each litany. It is to be repeated after each intention, even when it is not found printed in the text.

For the community to respond with true unity, it is preferable that it sing the response. Toward the end of the book, on pages 304-309, can be found the melodies for all the responses listed in alphabetical order.

6. Final orations

These prayers are said by the person who presides over the celebration. In some cases, the formulas presented are rather long. They can be shortened by omitting one or another part. The essential point is not to say everything, but to pray better.

7.   *Blessings and doxologies*

The liturgy prefers to conclude celebrations with the blessing, "May almighty God bless you, the Father, and the Son, and the Holy Spirit." These blessings of the assembly by God may be introduced by the assembly's blessing of God, i.e., by its giving praise and thanksgiving to God who blesses his people.

What is the purpose of these blessings in liturgical celebration?

The highest form of prayer is the doxology that praises the glory of God and the blessing that returns thanks to him. It is in our praise to God that we realize ourselves most fully, inasmuch as we become the living "praise of glory" (Ephesians 1:6,12), a calling we have received for all eternity.

This praise is found then at the heart of Christian prayer. It leads the community to that form of prayer that Jesus used in the hymn of jubilation (Matthew 11:25; see p.218), the most complete expression of his faith in the Father, "I bless you, Father, Lord of heaven and of earth!"

The Spirit of Jesus has devised all the formulas of praise that are offered here. It is also he who will create the praise in our prayer and will raise up in us a jubilant spirit.

You will find the blessings at the end of the section for each liturgical season: Advent (pp. 127-128), Christmas (p.141), Lent (pp. 158-159), Easter (pp. 175-176), and for All Seasons (pp. 298-302).

PART ONE

OPENING HYMNS

Glorify the Lord with me.
Let us praise his name.   *Ps 34*

O Lord, open my lips,
and my mouth shall declare your praise.   *Ps 51*

I will bless you all my life.
In your name I will lift up my hands.   *Ps 63*

Come in, let us bow and bend low.
Let us kneel before our God.   *Ps 95*

Glory to the Father, and to the Son, and to the Holy Spirit.
As it was in the beginning, is now, and will be forever. Amen.

BLESSINGS

Blessed be you, Lord, God of tenderness and compassion,
    rich in kindness and faithfulness,
who keep us in your love forever. Amen.   *Ex 34:6-7*

May you be blessed, Lord Jesus,
who died for our sins,
and rose again for our life!
To you be glory forever! Amen.*   *Rom 4:25*

OPENING HYMNS

KEEP IN MIND

*Keep in mind that Jesus Christ has died for us
and is risen from the dead.
He is our saving Lord, he is joy for all ages.*

    If we die with the Lord,
    we shall live with the Lord.
    If we endure with the Lord,
    we shall reign with the Lord.

    In him all our sorrow,
    in him all our joy.
    In him hope of glory,
    in him all our love.

    In him our redemption,
    in him all our grace.
    In him our salvation,
    in him all our peace.

---

*For other blessings, see pages 298-302.

ALL THE EARTH, PROCLAIM THE LORD

All the earth, proclaim the Lord,
Sing your praise to God.

Serve you the Lord, hearts filled with gladness.
Come into his presence singing for joy!

Know that the Lord is our creator.
Yes, he is our Father; we are his sons.

We are the sheep of his green pasture,
for we are his people; he is our God.

Enter his gates bringing thanksgiving,
O enter his courts while singing his praise.

Our Lord is good, his love enduring,
his word is abiding now with all men.

Honor and praise be to the Father,
the Son, and the Spirit, world without end.

JOY-GIVING LIGHT

Joy-giving light of the holy glory
of the heavenly and immortal Father,
holy and blessed Jesus Christ.

We gather at the close of day
beholding the evening light.
We praise the Father through the Son
in the holy Spirit of God.

At all times, O Lord,
you are worthy of praise with holy songs;
Son of God, Giver of life,
the world gives glory to you.

THERE IS ONE LORD

There is one Lord, there is one faith,
there is one baptism, one God,
who is Father.

We were called to be one in the Spirit of God,
  in the bond of peace.
  We sing and we proclaim.

We were called to form one body
  in one spirit.
  We sing and we proclaim.

We were called in the same hope
  in Christ the Lord.
  We sing and we proclaim.

AWAKE AND LIVE

Awake and live, O you who sleep,
awake and rise from the dead.
Let the light of Christ shine on you!

Baptized in your death
  and raised to life in your glory,
  we sing to you, Jesus Christ:
You open our lips and we praise your holy name;
teach us, O Lord, how to pray to God the Father.

Baptized in your death
  and raised to life in your glory,
  we sing to you, Jesus Christ:
Our souls are adorned for the splendor yet to come;
you are the way that will lead us to heaven.

Baptized in your death
  and raised to life in your glory,
  we sing to you, Jesus Christ:
Your life-giving word is now written on our hearts;
you are the promise the Father has given.

YOU SHALL LOVE THE LORD

You shall love the Lord, your God,
with all your heart, with all your mind,
with all your spirit, with all your power.
You shall love your neighbor as you love yourself.

Israel, hear: The Lord, he is your God;
he alone is Lord.

You shall love him with all your heart,
love him with all your soul,
love him with all your might.

YOU ARE THE HONOR

You are the honor, you are the glory of our people,
Holy Virgin Mary.

You are the glory of Jerusalem,
Holy Virgin Mary.

You are the greatest joy of Israel,
Holy Virgin Mary.

You are the highest honor of our race,
Holy Virgin Mary.

You are the honor, you are the glory of our people,
Holy Virgin Mary.

May you be blessed by the Lord most high,
Holy Virgin Mary.

Now, and for all ages without end,
Holy Virgin Mary.

Give praise to God in the Church, and Christ,
Holy Virgin Mary.

You are the honor, you are the glory of our people,
Holy Virgin Mary.

PART TWO

PSALMS
AND
CANTICLES

HAVING SPURNED THE LYRE AND THE HARP,
INSTRUMENTS WITHOUT SOUL,
JESUS, THE WORD OF GOD, HAS TUNED TO HIMSELF,
THROUGH THE HOLY SPIRIT,
THIS UNIVERSE AND ESPECIALLY MAN,
BODY AND SOUL,
WHO IS LIKE A LITTLE COSMOS.
HE SINGS TO HIS FATHER
WITH THIS INSTRUMENT OF A THOUSAND VOICES.
HE ACCOMPANIES HIS PRAISE
WITH THIS HARP, WHICH IS MAN.

Clement of Alexandria, *Protreptikos (An Exhortation to the Greeks)* I, 5, 3 .

IN PEACE I SLEEP

When I call, answer me, O God of justice;
from anguish you released me, have mercy and hear me!

O men, how long will your hearts be closed,
will you love what is futile and seek what is false?

It is the Lord who grants favors to those whom he loves;
the Lord hears me whenever I call him.

Fear him; do not sin: ponder on your bed and be still.
Make justice your sacrifice and trust in the Lord.

"What can bring us happiness?" many say.
Lift up the light of your face on us, O Lord.

You have put into my heart a greater joy
than they have from abundance of corn and new wine.

I will lie down in peace and sleep comes at once,
for you alone, Lord, make me dwell in safety.

God our Father,
when your Son Jesus Christ
fell asleep in suffering on the cross,
you released him from the anguish of death
and raised him from the tomb.
We implore you:
Reassure us when night enters our hearts.
Let the light of the face of the risen Lord
shine on our faces;
then we will await in trust and peace
the joy of that eternal day
when we will arise with your Son Jesus Christ,
our Savior and our brother,
forever and ever.

CHILDREN OF LIGHT   *1 Thessalonians 5:5, 9-10*
All of you are children of light, children of the day. We are not of the night, nor of
the darkness.... God has not destined us for wrath, but for acquiring salvation
through our Lord Jesus Christ. He died for us, so that, whether awake or asleep,
we will live together with him.

IN THE MORNING I OFFER YOU MY PRAYER

To my words give ear, O Lord,
give heed to my groaning.
Attend to the sound of my cries,
my King and my God.

It is you whom I invoke, O Lord.
In the morning you hear me;
in the morning I offer you my prayer,
watching and waiting.

You are no God who loves evil;
no sinner is your guest.
The boastful shall not stand their ground
before your face....

But I through the greatness of your love
have access to your house.
I bow down before your holy temple,
filled with awe.

Lead me, Lord, in your justice,
because of those who lie in wait;
make clear your way before me....

All those you protect shall be glad
and ring out their joy.
You shelter them; in you they rejoice,
those who love your name.

It is you who bless the just man, Lord:
you surround him with favor as with a shield.

In this morning, Lord our God,
we offer you our prayer.
May each day bring us nearer
to the great day
that knows no evening.
Then, through the greatness of your love,
we will have access to your eternal kingdom.

BEFORE GOD'S THRONE   *Revelation 7:14-15, 17*
These are the ones who came out of the great tribulation. They cleaned their
robes and made them white in the blood of the Lamb. Therefore they stand
before the throne of God. They serve him day and night in his temple.... He will
lead them to springs of living water. God will wipe away every tear from their
eyes.

HOW GREAT IS YOUR NAME!

How great is your name, O Lord our God,
through all the earth!

Your majesty is praised above the heavens;
on the lips of children and of babes
you have found praise to foil your enemy,
to silence the foe and the rebel.

When I see the heavens, the work of your hands,
the moon and the stars which you arranged,
what is man that you should keep him in mind,
mortal man that you care for him?

Yet you have made him little less than a god;
with glory and honor you crowned him,
gave him power over the works of your hand,
put all things under his feet.

All of them, sheep and cattle,
yes, even the savage beasts,
birds of the air, and fish
that make their way through the waters.

How great is your name, O Lord our God,
through all the earth!

Blessed indeed is your holy name, Lord our God,
for the birds of the air, for the fish in the sea,
for the flowers of the fields, for the fruits of the garden!
Blessed is your holy name
for the smile of our babies,
for the strength of our boys, the grace of our girls!
Blessed above all are you, Lord and Father,
for your Son Jesus Christ, the firstborn of all creatures,
our Savior and our brother, forever and ever.

JESUS IN PSALM 8   *1 Corinthians 15:20, 24-28*
Christ is now raised from the dead, the first fruits of all who have fallen asleep....
He will hand over the kingdom to God the Father, after destroying every sovereignty, every authority and power. For he must reign until

he has put all his enemies
under his feet.

The last enemy to be destroyed is death. When all things have been subjected to him, the Son himself will also be subject to God the Father, who put all things under him, so then God will be all in all.

THE LORD, MY HERITAGE

Preserve me, God, I take refuge in you.
I say to the Lord: "You are my God.
My happiness lies in you alone."

He has put into my heart a marvelous love
for the faithful ones who dwell in his land.
Those who choose other gods increase their sorrows.
Never will I offer their offerings of blood.
Never will I take their name upon my lips.

O Lord, it is you who are my portion and cup;
it is you yourself who are my prize.
The lot marked out for me is my delight:
welcome indeed the heritage that falls to me!

I will bless the Lord who gives me counsel,
who even at night directs my heart.
I keep the Lord ever in my sight:
since he is at my right hand, I shall stand firm.

And so my heart rejoices, my soul is glad;
even my body shall rest in safety.
For you will not leave my soul among the dead,
nor let your beloved know decay.

You will show me the path of life,
the fullness of joy in your presence,
at your right hand happiness forever.

We bless you, Lord Jesus Christ!
Our happiness lies in you alone.
Do not abandon the ones you love.
When the night of our death comes,
place us at your right hand,
where we will find gladness forever and ever.

JESUS IN PSALM 16   *Acts 2:22...36*
Jesus the Nazorean was a man whom God sent to you. You killed him, but God
raised him to life. He freed him from the bitter pangs of death, for it was
impossible for him to be held in its power. David says of him:

> *You will not abandon my soul to the nether world*
> *nor suffer your faithful one to undergo corruption.*

God raised this man Jesus to life, and all of us are witnesses to that. Exalted at
God's right hand, he has received from the Father the Holy Spirit, who was
promised. Therefore, let the whole house of Israel be certain that God has made
this Jesus whom you crucified both LORD and CHRIST.

THE LAW OF GOD IS PERFECT

The law of the Lord is perfect,
it revives the soul.
The rule of the Lord is to be trusted,
it gives wisdom to the simple.

The precepts of the Lord are right,
they gladden the heart.
The command of the Lord is clear,
it gives light to the eyes.

The fear of the Lord is holy,
abiding forever.
The decrees of the Lord are truth
and all of them just.

They are more to be desired than gold,
than the purest of gold
and sweeter are they than honey,
than honey from the comb.

So in them your servant finds instruction;
great reward is in their keeping.
But who can detect all his errors?
From hidden faults acquit me.

From presumption restrain your servant
and let it not rule me.
Then shall I be blameless,
clean from grave sin.

May the spoken words of my mouth,
the thoughts of my heart,
win favor in your sight, O Lord,
my rescuer, my rock!

God our Father,
your Word is your Son, Jesus Christ.
He is light for our eyes and joy for our souls.
May he always dwell in our hearts.

THE WORD OF GOD   *Hebrews 4:12-13*
Indeed, the Word of God is living and active, sharper than any two-edged sword.
It pierces, dividing soul from spirit, joints from marrow. It judges the thoughts
and intentions of the heart. No creature can be concealed before him. All things
are uncovered and exposed to his eyes. To him we must render an account.

SUFFERING AND TRIUMPH OF THE JUST

My God, my God, why have you forsaken me?
You are far from my plea and the cry of my distress.
O my God, I call by day and you give no reply;
I call by night and I find no peace.

Yet you, O God, are holy,
enthroned on the praises of Israel.
In you our fathers put their trust;
they trusted and you set them free.
When they cried to you, they escaped.
In you they trusted and never in vain.

But I am a worm and no man,
the butt of men, laughingstock of the people.
All who see me deride me.
They curl their lips, they toss their heads.
"He trusted in the Lord, let him save him;
let him release him if this is his friend."

Yes, it was you who took me from the womb,
entrusted me to my mother's breast.
To you I was committed from my birth,
from my mother's womb you have been my God.
Do not leave me alone in my distress;
come close, there is none else to help.

Many bulls have surrounded me,
fierce bulls of Bashan close me in.
Against me they open wide their jaws,
like lions, rending and roaring.

Like water I am poured out,
disjointed are all my bones.
My heart has become like wax,
it is melted within my breast.
Parched as burnt clay is my throat,
my tongue cleaves to my jaws.

Many dogs have surrounded me,
a band of the wicked beset me.
They tear holes in my hands and my feet
and lay me in the dust of death.

I can count every one of my bones.
These people stare at me and gloat;
they divide my clothing among them.
They cast lots for my robe.

JESUS IN PSALM 22   *Matthew 27:45-46*
From the sixth hour darkness came over the whole land until the ninth hour.
Then, about the ninth hour, Jesus cried out in a loud voice, *"Eli, Eli, lema
sabachthani?"*, which means, *"My God, my God, why have you forsaken me?"*

O Lord, do not leave me alone,
my strength, make haste to help me!
Rescue my soul from the sword,
my life from the grip of these dogs.
Save my life from the jaws of these lions,
my poor soul from the horns of these oxen.

I will tell of your name to my brethren
and praise you where they are assembled.
"You who fear the Lord give him praise;
all sons of Jacob, give him glory.
Revere him, Israel's sons.

For he has never despised
nor scorned the poverty of the poor.
From him he has not hidden his face,
but he heard the poor man when he cried."

You are my praise in the great assembly.
My vows I will pay before those who fear him.
The poor shall eat and shall have their fill.
They shall praise the Lord, those who seek him.
May their hearts live forever and ever!

All the earth shall remember and return to the Lord,
all families of the nations worship before him
for the kingdom is the Lord's; he is ruler of the nations.
They shall worship him, all the mighty of the earth;
before him shall bow all who go down to the dust.

And my soul shall live for him, my children serve him.
They shall tell of the Lord to generations yet to come,
declare his faithfulness to peoples yet unborn:
"These things the Lord has done."*

JESUS IN PSALM 22   *Hebrews 2:11-12, 17*
Jesus is not ashamed to call them brethren, saying:

> *I will tell of your name to my brethren,*
> *I will praise you in the midst of the assembly.*

He had to become in every way like his brethren, so that he might be a merciful and trustworthy priest before God on their behalf, to expiate the sins of the people.

*See the prayer, "Father of Jesus," p. 153.

THE LORD IS MY SHEPHERD

The Lord is my shepherd;
there is nothing I shall want.
Fresh and green are the pastures
where he gives me repose.

Near restful waters he leads me,
to revive my drooping spirit.

He guides me along the right path;
he is true to his name.

If I should walk in the valley of darkness
no evil would I fear.
You are there with your crook and your staff;
with these you give me comfort.

You have prepared a banquet for me
in the sight of my foes.
My head you have anointed with oil;
my cup is overflowing.

Surely goodness and kindness shall follow me
all the days of my life.
In the Lord's own house shall I dwell
forever and ever.

Blessed are you, Lord Jesus Christ,
Good Shepherd of your Church!
In our baptism you anointed us
with the oil of salvation,
and in the eucharist you spread before us
the table of your heavenly bread.
Lead us by your goodness and kindness
through the dark valley of death
to the day when we will dwell forever
in the house of your Father.

JESUS, THE GOOD SHEPHERD   *John 10:14-16*
"I am the good shepherd. I know my sheep and my sheep know me, just as the
Father knows me and I know the Father. I give my life for my sheep. I have other
sheep that are not of this fold. I have to lead them also. They shall hear my voice.
There shall be one flock and one shepherd."

THE LORD, THE KING OF GLORY

The Lord's is the earth and its fullness,
the world and all its peoples.
It is he who set it on the seas;
on the waters he made it firm.

Who shall climb the mountain of the Lord?
Who shall stand in his holy place?
The man with clean hands and pure heart,
who desires not worthless things,
who has not sworn so as to deceive his neighbor.

He shall receive blessings from the Lord
and reward from the God who saves him.
Such are the men who seek him,
seek the face of the God of Jacob.

O gates, lift high your heads;
grow higher, ancient doors.
Let him enter, the king of glory!

Who is the king of glory?
The Lord, the mighty, the valiant,
the Lord, the valiant in war.

O gates, lift high your heads;
grow higher, ancient doors.
Let him enter, the king of glory!

Who is he, the king of glory?
He, the Lord of armies,
he is the king of glory.

Lord God our Father,
almighty and eternal king of glory,
open for us the gates of the new Jerusalem.

With sinless hands and clean hearts
may we, with Christ, ascend your holy mountain,
where we will encounter your infinite tenderness,
forever and ever.

CHRIST IN HEAVEN   *Hebrews 9:15, 24*
Christ is the mediator of a new covenant.... He did not enter into a sanctuary
made by hands, which is only a copy of the true one, but he entered into heaven
itself, now to stand in the presence of God on our behalf.

HIS WAYS ARE FAITHFULNESS AND LOVE

To you, O Lord, I lift up my soul.
I trust you, let me not be disappointed;
do not let my enemies triumph.
Those who hope in you shall not be disappointed,
but only those who wantonly break faith.

Lord, make me know your ways.
Lord, teach me your paths.
Make me walk in your truth, and teach me:
for you are God my savior.

In you I hope all day long
because of your goodness, O Lord.
Remember your mercy, Lord,
and the love you have shown from of old.
Do not remember the sins of my youth.
In your love remember me.

The Lord is good and upright.
He shows the path to those who stray,
he guides the humble in the right path;
he teaches his way to the poor.

His ways are faithfulness and love
for those who keep his covenant and will.
Lord, for the sake of your name,
forgive my guilt; for it is great.

If anyone fears the Lord,
he will show him the path he should choose.
His soul shall live in happiness
and his children shall possess the land.
The Lord's friendship is for those who revere him;
to them he reveals his covenant.

My eyes are always on the Lord;
for he rescues my feet from the snare.
Turn to me and have mercy
for I am lonely and poor.

Relieve the anguish of my heart
and set me free from my distress.
See my affliction and my toil
and take all my sins away.

See how many are my foes;
how violent their hatred for me.

GOD'S LOVE AMONG US   *1 John 4:9-10*
In this the love of God was made manifest among us: God sent his only Son into
the world, so that we could live through him. Love consists in this: not that we
loved God, but that he loved us and sent his Son as an offering for our sins.

Preserve my life and rescue me.
Do not disappoint me, you are my refuge.
May innocence and uprightness protect me:
for my hope is in you, O Lord.

Redeem Israel, O God, from all its distress.

God our Father, through your Spirit
you assure us in this psalm
that all your ways are faithfulness and love.
Help us to understand, we beg you,
that these words are true,
and that each step on the road of life
brings us nearer to the eternal kingdom of your love.

PSALM 27

THE LORD IS MY LIGHT AND MY HELP

The Lord is my light and my help;
whom shall I fear?
The Lord is the stronghold of my life;
before whom shall I shrink?

When evildoers draw near
to devour my flesh,
it is they, my enemies and foes,
who stumble and fall.

Though an army encamp against me
my heart would not fear.
Though war break out against me
even then would I trust.

There is one thing I ask of the Lord,
for this I long,
to live in the house of the Lord,
all the days of my life,
to savor the sweetness of the Lord,
to behold his temple.

For there he keeps me safe in his tent
in the day of evil.
He hides me in the shelter of his tent,
on a rock he sets me safe.

And now my head shall be raised
above my foes who surround me
and I shall offer within his tent
a sacrifice of joy.

I will sing and make music for the Lord.

O Lord, hear my voice when I call;
have mercy and answer.
Of you my heart has spoken:
"Seek his face."

It is your face, O Lord, that I seek;
hide not your face.
Dismiss not your servant in anger;
you have been my help.

Do not abandon or forsake me,
O God my help!
Though father and mother forsake me,
the Lord will receive me.

Instruct me, Lord, in your way;
on an even path lead me.
When they lie in ambush protect me
from my enemy's greed.
False witnesses rise against me,
breathing out fury.

I am sure I shall see the Lord's goodness
in the land of the living.
Hope in him, hold firm and take heart.
Hope in the Lord!

Father of light and Savior of the poor,
source of all joy and fountain of peace,
we seek your face!
When we cry to you,
recognize in our voices
the voice of your beloved Son.
He is our Savior and brother
forever and ever.

JESUS, LIGHT OF THE WORLD   *John 8:12*
"I am the light of the world. Who follows me shall never walk in darkness, but
shall possess the light of life."

FATHER, INTO YOUR HANDS I COMMEND MY SPIRIT

In you, O Lord, I take refuge.
Let me never be put to shame.
In your justice, set me free,
hear me and speedily rescue me.

Be a rock of refuge for me,
a mighty stronghold to save me,
for you are my rock, my stronghold.
For your name's sake, lead me and guide me.

Release me from the snares they have hidden
for you are my refuge, Lord.
Into your hands I commend my spirit.
It is you who will redeem me, Lord.

O God of truth, you detest
those who worship false and empty gods.
As for me, I trust in the Lord:
let me be glad and rejoice in your love.

You, who have seen my affliction
and taken heed of my soul's distress,
have not handed me over to the enemy,
but set my feet at large....

How great is the goodness, Lord,
that you keep for those who fear you,
that you show to those who trust you
in the sight of men.

You hide them in the shelter of your presence
from the plotting of men:
you keep them safe within your tent
from disputing tongues.

Blessed be the Lord who has shown me
the wonders of his love
in a fortified city.

"I am far removed from your sight,"
I said in my alarm.
Yet you heard the voice of my plea
when I cried for help.

JESUS IN PSALM 31   *Luke 23:44-47*
From about midday until midafternoon the sun stopped shining and darkness
came over the whole land. The curtain in the sanctuary was torn in two. Jesus
uttered a loud cry and said:

Father, into your hands I commend my spirit.

After he said this, he expired. The centurion, upon seeing what had happened,
gave glory to God by saying, "Surely, this was an innocent man."

Love the Lord, all you saints.
He guards his faithful
but the Lord will repay to the full
those who act with pride.

Be strong, let your heart take courage,
all who hope in the Lord.

Blessed are you, Lord my God,
because you created me!
Into your hands, with your Son, Jesus Christ,
I commend my spirit.
Show me the wonders of your love
in the city of your eternal gladness.

PSALM 32

YES, I SHALL ARISE AND RETURN TO MY FATHER

Happy the man whose offense is forgiven, whose sin is remitted.
O happy the man to whom the Lord imputes no guilt,
in whose spirit is no guile.

I kept it secret and my frame was wasted.
I groaned all the day long
for night and day your hand was heavy upon me....

But now I have acknowledged my sins;
my guilt I did not hide.
I said: "I will confess my offense to the Lord."
And you, Lord, have forgiven
the guilt of my sin.

So let every good man pray to you in the time of need.
The floods of water may reach high
but him they shall not reach.
You are my hiding place, O Lord;
you save me from distress.
You surround me with cries of deliverance.

I will instruct you and teach you
the way you should go;
I will give you counsel with my eye upon you....

THE SON WHO WAS LOST AND IS FOUND   *Luke 15:18, 23-24*
"I shall arise and return to my father and say to him, 'Father, I have sinned
against God and against you....' "
The father said, "Let us eat and celebrate because this son of mine was dead and
has come back to life. He was lost and is found."

Rejoice, rejoice in the Lord,
exult, you just!
O come, ring out your joy,
all you upright of heart.

Who is like you, God our Father,
who removes guilt and pardons sins,
who delights in showing mercy?
Again, have pity on us,
give us the joy of your forgiveness,
in the name of your beloved Son, Jesus Christ,
our Savior and our brother, forever and ever.

PSALM 33

HE FILLS THE EARTH WITH HIS KINDNESS

Ring out your joy to the Lord, O you just;
for praise is fitting for loyal hearts.

Give thanks to the Lord upon the harp,
with a ten-stringed lute sing him songs.
O sing him a song that is new,
play loudly, with all your skill.

For the word of the Lord is faithful
and all his works to be trusted.
The Lord loves justice and right
and fills the earth with his love.

By his word the heavens were made,
by the breath of his mouth all the stars.
He collects the waves of the ocean;
he stores up the depths of the sea.

Let all the earth fear the Lord,
all who live in the world revere him.
He spoke; and it came to be.
He commanded; it sprang into being.

He frustrates the designs of the nations,
he defeats the plans of the peoples.
His own designs shall stand forever,
the plans of his heart from age to age.

GOD'S LOVE ON EARTH　　　　　　　　　　　　*Romans 5:5, 8*
The love of God has been poured out into our hearts through the Holy Spirit who
has been given to us.... God proves his love for us in that while we were still
sinners Christ died for us.

They are happy, whose God is the Lord,
the people he has chosen as his own.
From the heavens the Lord looks forth,
he sees all the children of men.

From the place where he dwells he gazes
on all the dwellers on the earth,
he who shapes the hearts of them all
and considers all their deeds....

The Lord looks on those who revere him,
on those who hope in his love,
to rescue their souls from death,
to keep them alive in famine.

Our soul is waiting for the Lord.
The Lord is our help and our shield.
In him do our hearts find joy.
We trust in his holy name.

May your love be upon us, O Lord,
as we place all our hope in you.

God our Father,
your love fills the earth,
your love fills our life,
your love will fill our eternity,
*Blessed are you eternally!**

---

*See also the prayer, "May Your Kindness, O Lord," p. 265.

I WILL BLESS THE LORD AT ALL TIMES

I will bless the Lord at all times,
his praise always on my lips;
in the Lord my soul shall make its boast.
The humble shall hear and be glad.

Glorify the Lord with me.
Together let us praise his name.
I sought the Lord and he answered me;
from all my terrors he set me free.

Look towards him and be radiant;
let your faces not be abashed.
This poor man called; the Lord heard him
and rescued him from all his distress.

The angel of the Lord is encamped
around those who revere him, to rescue them.
Taste and see that the Lord is good.
He is happy who seeks refuge in him.

Revere the Lord, you his saints.
They lack nothing, those who revere him.
Strong lions suffer want and go hungry
but those who seek the Lord lack no blessing.

Come, children, and hear me
that I may teach you the fear of the Lord.
Who is he who longs for life
and many days, to enjoy his prosperity?

Then keep your tongue from evil
and your lips from speaking deceit.
Turn aside from evil and do good;
seek and strive after peace.

The Lord turns his face against the wicked
to destroy their remembrance from the earth.
The Lord turns his eyes to the just
and his ears to their appeal.

They call and the Lord hears
and rescues them in all their distress.
The Lord is close to the brokenhearted;
those whose spirit is crushed he will save.

Many are the trials of the just man
but from them all the Lord will rescue him.

GIVE THANKS TO GOD   *Colossians 3:16-17*
In psalms, hymns, and inspired songs, sing with thankfulness to God in your
hearts. And whatever you do, whether in word or in deed, do everything in the
name of the Lord Jesus, giving thanks to God the Father through him.

He will keep guard over all his bones,
not one of his bones shall be broken.

Evil brings death to the wicked;
those who hate the good are doomed.

We thank you, God our Father,
because you accept the song of our praise,
because you hear the call of our suffering,
because your angel rescues us from the prison of distress.
We thank you especially because you are our God
and we are your children,
through Jesus Christ, forever and ever.

PSALM 40

HERE I AM TO DO YOUR WILL

I waited, I waited for the Lord
and he stooped down to me;
he heard my cry.

He drew me from the deadly pit,
from the miry clay.
He set my feet upon a rock
and made my footsteps firm.

He put a new song into my mouth,
praise of our God.
Many shall see and fear
and shall trust in the Lord.

Happy the man who has placed
his trust in the Lord
and has not gone over to the rebels
who follow false gods.

JESUS CHRIST IN PSALM 40   *Hebrews 10:1...10*
The law is incapable of bringing the worshipers to perfection with the same
sacrifices continually offered year after year. Coming into the world, Jesus
Christ said:

Sacrifices and oblations you did not want,
but a body you prepared for me.
In holocausts or victims you did not take pleasure.
Then I said, "God, here I am to do your will,
as it stands written of me in the scroll of the book."

Thus, by that will we have been sanctified by the offering of the body of Jesus
Christ once for all.

How many, O Lord my God,
are the wonders and designs
that you have worked for us;
you have no equal.
Should I proclaim and speak of them,
they are more than I can tell!

You do not ask for sacrifice and offerings,
but an open ear.
You do not ask for holocaust and victim.
Instead, here am I.

In the scroll of the book it stands written
that I should do your will.
My God, I delight in your law
in the depth of my heart.

Your justice I have proclaimed
in the great assembly.
My lips I have not sealed;
you know it, O Lord.

I have not hidden your justice in my heart
but declared your faithful help.
I have not hidden your love and your truth
from the great assembly.

O Lord, you will not withhold
your compassion from me.
Your merciful love and your truth
will always guard me....

O let there be rejoicing and gladness
for all who seek you.
Let them ever say: "The Lord is great,"
who love your saving help.

As for me, wretched and poor,
the Lord thinks of me.
You are my rescuer, my help,
O God, do not delay.

Lord Jesus Christ, our saving Lord,
you came into our world
to fulfill the will of your Father
and became obedient unto death,
even death on a cross.
We ask you:
Teach us to follow the Father's will always
and to discover in it his great love,
for our greater joy and heavenly peace.

LIKE THE DEER

Like the deer that yearns
for running streams,
so my soul is yearning
for you, my God.

My soul is thirsting for God,
the God of my life;
when can I enter and see
the face of God?

My tears have become my bread,
by night, by day,
as I hear it said all the day long:
"Where is your God?"

These things will I remember
as I pour out my soul:
how I would lead the rejoicing crowd
into the house of God,
amid cries of gladness and thanksgiving,
the throng wild with joy.

Why are you cast down, my soul,
why groan within me?
Hope in God; I will praise him still,
my savior and my God.

My soul is cast down within me
as I think of you,
from the country of Jordan and Mount Hermon,
from the Hill of Mizar.

Deep is calling on deep,
in the roar of waters:
your torrents and all your waves
swept over me.

By day the Lord will send
his loving-kindness;
by night I will sing to him,
praise the God of my life.

I will say to God, my rock:
"Why have you forgotten me?
Why do I go mourning
oppressed by the foe?"

With cries that pierce me to the heart,
my enemies revile me,
saying to me all the day long:
"Where is your God?"

LIVING WATER FOR ETERNAL LIFE   *John 4:14*
"The water I give shall become in him a spring welling up to eternal life."

Why are you cast down, my soul,
why groan within me?
Hope in God; I will praise him still,
my savior and my God.

(PSALM 43)

Defend me, O God, and plead my cause
against a godless nation.
From deceitful and cunning men
rescue me, O God.

Since you, O God, are my stronghold,
why have you rejected me?
Why do I go mourning
oppressed by the foe?

O send forth your light and your truth;
let these be my guide.
Let them bring me to your holy mountain
to the place where you dwell.

And I will come to the altar of God,
the God of my joy.
My redeemer, I will thank you on the harp,
O God, my God.

Why are you cast down, my soul,
why groan within me?
Hope in God; I will praise him still,
my savior and my God.

God of my life and song of my joy,
when can I see your face?
Send forth your light and your truth,
your Son Jesus Christ.
May he guide us amid cries of gladness
into the house where you dwell,
God of my life and song of my joy!

GOD IS KING OF ALL THE EARTH

All peoples, clap your hands,
cry to God with shouts of joy!
For the Lord, the Most High, we must fear,
great king over all the earth.

He subdues peoples under us
and nations under our feet.
Our inheritance, our glory, is from him,
given to Jacob out of love.

God goes up with shouts of joy;
the Lord goes up with trumpet blast.
Sing praise for God, sing praise,
sing praise to our king, sing praise.

God is king of all the earth.
Sing praise with all your skill.
God is king over the nations;
God reigns on his holy throne.

The princes of the peoples are assembled
with the people of Abraham's God.
The rulers of the earth belong to God,
to God who reigns over all.

Lord Jesus Christ,
great King over all the earth,
you are glorified in heaven
while you remain our brother on earth.
You reign from your holy throne
while you abide in the hearts of the poor.
You are acclaimed with cries of joy by the angels
while you accept the prayer of our pain.
We bless you and give you glory.
The power of your realm
is the power of your love,
and the praise of your strength
is the song of your kindness,
which endures forever and ever.

JESUS CHRIST THE LORD   *Mark 16:15, 19*
"Go out to the whole world. Proclaim the Good News to all creation...." Then the
Lord Jesus was taken up into heaven and took his seat at God's right hand.

HAVE MERCY ON ME, GOD

Have mercy on me, God, in your kindness.
In your compassion blot out my offense.
O wash me more and more from my guilt
and cleanse me from my sin.

My offenses truly I know them;
my sin is always before me.
Against you, you alone, have I sinned;
what is evil in your sight I have done.

That you may be justified when you give sentence
and be without reproach when you judge,
O see, in guilt I was born,
a sinner was I conceived.

Indeed you love truth in the heart;
then in the secret of my heart teach me wisdom.
O purify me, then I shall be clean;
O wash me, I shall be whiter than snow.

Make me hear rejoicing and gladness,
that the bones you have crushed may thrill.
From my sins turn away your face
and blot out all my guilt.

A pure heart create for me, O God,
put a steadfast spirit within me.
Do not cast me away from your presence,
nor deprive me of your holy spirit.

Give me again the joy of your help;
with a spirit of fervor sustain me,
that I may teach transgressors your ways
and sinners may return to you.

O rescue me, God, my helper,
and my tongue shall ring out your goodness.
O Lord, open my lips
and my mouth shall declare your praise.

For in sacrifice you take no delight,
burnt offering from me you would refuse,
my sacrifice, a contrite spirit.
A humbled, contrite heart you will not spurn.

In your goodness, show favor to Zion:
rebuild the walls of Jerusalem.

GOD, BE MERCIFUL TO ME   *Luke 18:13*
"The tax collector stood far away, not daring even to raise his eyes to heaven. He
beat his breast, saying, 'O God, be merciful to me, a sinner.'"

Then you will be pleased with lawful sacrifice,
burnt offerings wholly consumed.

God our Father,
Lord of all mercy and all pardons,
through the greatness of your compassion,
create a clean heart in us,
and renew a steadfast spirit in us.
Give us the Spirit of your own Son Jesus Christ,
so that our lips, closed by our sins,
will open to proclaim your praise
forever and ever.

PSALM 57

AWAKE MY SOUL

O God, arise above the heavens;
may your glory shine on earth!...

My heart is ready, O God,
my heart is ready.
I will sing, I will sing your praise.
Awake my soul,
awake lyre and harp,
I will awake the dawn.

I will thank you, Lord, among the peoples,
among the nations I will praise you,
for your love reaches to the heavens
and your truth to the skies.

O God, arise above the heavens;
may your glory shine on earth!

Awake my soul, O Lord my God.
Make of my life
a song of joy
in Jesus Christ!

YOUR LOVE IS BETTER THAN LIFE

O God, you are my God, for you I long;
for you my soul is thirsting.
My body pines for you
like a dry, weary land without water.
So I gaze on you in the sanctuary
to see your strength and your glory.

For your love is better than life,
my lips will speak your praise.
So I will bless you all my life,
in your name I will lift up my hands.
My soul shall be filled as with a banquet,
my mouth shall praise you with joy.

On my bed I remember you.
On you I muse through the night
for you have been my help;
in the shadow of your wings I rejoice.
My soul clings to you;
your right hand holds me fast....

PSALM 65

SONG OF SPRINGTIME

To you our praise is due
in Zion, O God.
To you we pay our vows,
you who hear our prayer.

To you all flesh will come
with its burden of sin.
Too heavy for us, our offenses,
but you wipe them away.

Blessed is he whom you choose and call
to dwell in your courts.
We are filled with the blessings of your house,
of your holy temple.

You keep your pledge with wonders,
O God our savior,
the hope of all the earth
and of far distant isles.

MY BURDEN IS LIGHT   *Matthew 11:28-30*
"Come to me all you who labor and are burdened, and I will give you rest. Take
up my yoke upon you and learn from me, for I am gentle and humble of heart.
You will find rest for your souls, for my yoke is easy and my burden light."

You uphold the mountains with your strength,
you are girded with power.
You still the roaring of the seas,
the roaring of their waves,
and the tumult of the peoples.

The ends of the earth stand in awe
at the sight of your wonders.
The lands of sunrise and sunset
you fill with your joy.

You care for the earth, give it water,
you fill it with riches.
Your river in heaven brims over
to provide its grain.

And thus you provide for the earth;
you drench its furrows,
you level it, soften it with showers,
you bless its growth.

You crown the year with your goodness.
Abundance flows in your steps,
in the pastures of the wilderness it flows.

The hills are girded with joy,
the meadows covered with flocks,
the valleys are decked with wheat.
They shout for joy, yes, they sing.

Lord Jesus Christ, you are the springtime of our life.
You garment the fields of the Church with the sod of your Word,
and you blanket the valleys of our sins with your grace.
We pray to you:
Continue to crown the year with your bounty;
and when we are overcome by our sins,
cover us with your mercy.

HARVEST SONG

O God, be gracious and bless us
and let your face shed its light upon us.
So will your ways be known upon earth
and all nations learn your saving help.

Let the peoples praise you, O God;
let all the peoples praise you.

Let the nations be glad and exult
for you rule the world with justice.
With fairness you rule the peoples,
you guide the nations on earth.

Let the peoples praise you, O God;
let all the peoples praise you.

The earth has yielded its fruit
for God, our God, has blessed us.
May God still give us his blessing
till the ends of the earth revere him.

Let the peoples praise you, O God;
let all the peoples praise you.

May you be blessed, God our Father;
you open our lips to praise you.

While we stand in your presence,
let the light of your face shine upon us.

While our lips sing your praise,
let our hearts come nearer to you.

THE FIELDS ARE WHITE FOR HARVEST   *John 4:23-24, 35-36*
"An hour is coming and it is now when the true worshipers will worship the
Father in spirit and in truth. Indeed, the Father seeks such worshipers. God is
Spirit, and those who worship him must worship in spirit and in truth."
"Lift up your eyes and see! The fields are white for harvest. Already the reaper
receives his wages and gathers fruit for eternal life, so that the sower rejoices
together with the reaper."

GOD'S TRIUMPHAL PROCESSION

Let God arise, let his foes be scattered.
Let those who hate him flee before him.
As smoke is blown away so will they be blown away;
like wax that melts before the fire,
so the wicked shall perish at the presence of God.

But the just shall rejoice at the presence of God,
they shall exult and dance for joy.
O sing to the Lord, make music to his name;
make a highway for him who rides on the clouds.
Rejoice in the Lord, exult at his presence.

Father of the orphan, defender of the widow,
such is God in his holy place.
God gives the lonely a home to live in;
he leads the prisoners forth into freedom:
but rebels must dwell in a parched land.

When you went forth, O God, at the head of your people,
when you marched across the desert, the earth trembled:
the heavens melted at the presence of God,
at the presence of God, Israel's God.

You poured down, O God, a generous rain:
when your people were starved you gave them new life.
It was there that your people found a home,
prepared in your goodness, O God, for the poor....

The chariots of God are thousands upon thousands.
The Lord has come from Sinai to the holy place.
You have gone up on high; you have taken captives,
receiving men in tribute, O God,
even those who rebel, into your dwelling, O Lord.

May the Lord be blessed day after day.
He bears our burdens, God our savior.
This God of ours is a God who saves.
The Lord our God holds the keys of death....

They see your solemn procession, O God,
the procession of my God, of my king, to the sanctuary:

CHRIST IN PSALM 68   *Ephesians 4:7-8, 11-13*
Each one of us has been given God's grace, according to the measure of Christ's
gift. Therefore [the Scripture] says:

When he ascended on high, he took a host of captives,
and he gave gifts to men.

And these were his gifts: some to be apostles, some to be prophets, some to be
evangelists, some to be pastors, some to be teachers; they are for the perfection of
the saints, for the work of ministry, for building up the body of Christ, till we
become one in faith and in our knowledge of God's Son. Thus, we could form that
perfect Man who is Christ come to full stature.

the singers in the forefront, the musicians coming last,
between them, maidens sounding their timbrels.

"In festive gatherings, bless the Lord;
bless God, O you who are Israel's sons."
There is Benjamin, least of the tribes, at the head,
Judah's princes, a mighty throng,
Zebulun's princes, Naphtali's princes.

Show forth, O God, show forth your might,
your might, O God, which you have shown for us.
For the sake of your temple high in Jerusalem
may kings come to you bringing their tribute.

Threaten the wild beast that dwells in the reeds,
the bands of the mighty and lords of the peoples.
Let them bow down offering silver.
Scatter the peoples who delight in war.
Princes will make their way from Egypt:
Ethiopia will stretch out her hands to God.

Kingdoms of the earth, sing to God, praise the Lord
who rides on the heavens, the ancient heavens.
He thunders his voice, his mighty voice.
Come, acknowledge the power of God.

His glory is on Israel; his might is in the skies.
God is to be feared in his holy place.
He is the Lord, Israel's God.
He gives strength and power to his people.

Blessed be God!

How glorious were your processions, O God our Lord,
into your holy sanctuary in Jerusalem!
The singers in front, the musicians follow,
in their midst the maidens play on timbrels.
Why should our celebrations today be sad and boring?
Let the day come soon when our churches
will be filled with songs of gladness,
when our maidens will play timbrels of joy,
when your holy people will dance
to celebrate your love in Jesus Christ!

PRAYER IN GREAT DISTRESS

Save me, O God,
for the waters have risen to my neck.

I have sunk into the mud of the deep
and there is no foothold.
I have entered the waters of the deep
and the waves overwhelm me.

I am wearied with all my crying,
my throat is parched.
My eyes are wasted away
from looking for my God.

More numerous than the hairs on my head
are those who hate me without cause.
Those who attack me with lies
are too much for my strength.

How can I restore
what I have never stolen?
O God, you know my sinful folly;
my sins you can see.

Let those who hope in you not be put to shame
through me, Lord of hosts:
let not those who seek you be dismayed
through me, God of Israel.

It is for you that I suffer taunts,
that shame covers my face,
that I have become a stranger to my brothers,
an alien to my own mother's sons.
I burn with zeal for your house
and taunts against you fall on me.

When I afflict my soul with fasting
they make it a taunt against me.
When I put on sackcloth in mourning
then they make me a byword,
the gossip of men at the gates,
the subject of drunkards' songs.

This is my prayer to you,
my prayer for your favor.
In your great love, answer me, O God,
with your help that never fails:
rescue me from sinking in the mud;
save me from my foes.

JESUS IN PSALM 69 (Cleansing of the Temple)   *John 2:16-17*
"Do not turn my Father's house into a marketplace." His disciples remembered
that it was written, *"Zeal for your house consumes me."*

Save me from the waters of the deep
lest the waves overwhelm me.
Do not let the deep engulf me
nor death close its mouth on me.

Lord, answer, for your love is kind;
in your compassion, turn towards me.
Do not hide your face from your servant;
answer quickly for I am in distress....

Taunts have broken my heart;
I have reached the end of my strength.
I looked in vain for compassion,
for consolers; not one could I find.

For food they gave me poison;
in my thirst they gave me vinegar to drink....

As for me in my poverty and pain
let your help, O God, lift me up.

I will praise God's name with a song;
I will glorify him with thanksgiving.
A gift pleasing God more than oxen,
more than beasts prepared for sacrifice.

The poor when they see it will be glad
and God-seeking hearts will revive;
for the Lord listens to the needy
and does not spurn his servants in their chains.
Let the heavens and the earth give him praise,
the sea and all its living creatures.

For God will bring help to Zion
and rebuild the cities of Judah
and men shall dwell there in possession.
The sons of his servants shall inherit it;
those who love his name shall dwell there.

JESUS IN PSALM 69 (Prayer on the Cross)   *John 19:28, 30*
Knowing that all was now finished, Jesus said, to fulfill the Scripture, "I am
thirsty."... When he received the vinegar, he said, "It is finished." Then he bowed
his head and gave up his spirit.

PRAYER IN TIME OF OLD AGE

In you, O Lord, I take refuge;
let me never be put to shame.
In your justice rescue me, free me:
pay heed to me and save me.

Be a rock where I can take refuge,
a mighty stronghold to save me;
for you are my rock, my stronghold.
Free me from the hand of the wicked,
from the grip of the unjust, of the oppressor.

It is you, O Lord, who are my hope,
my trust, O Lord, since my youth.
On you I have leaned from my birth,
from my mother's womb you have been my help.
My hope has always been in you.

My fate has filled many with awe
but you are my strong refuge.
My lips are filled with your praise,
with your glory all the day long.
Do not reject me now that I am old;
when my strength fails do not forsake me.

For my enemies are speaking about me;
those who watch me take counsel together
saying: "God has forsaken him; follow him,
seize him; there is no one to save him."
O God, do not stay far off:
my God, make haste to help me!...

But as for me, I will always hope
and praise you more and more.
My lips will tell of your justice
and day by day of your help
though I can never tell it all.

I will declare the Lord's mighty deeds
proclaiming your justice, yours alone.
O God, you have taught me from my youth
and I proclaim your wonders still.

Now that I am old and grey-headed,
do not forsake me, God.

PRAYER OF SIMEON   *Luke 2:28-30, 32*
Simeon took Jesus up in his arms. He blessed God and said, "Now, Master, you
can let your servant, following your words, go in peace. For my eyes have seen
your salvation...a light for revelation to the nations and for glory to your people
Israel."

Let me tell of your power to all ages,
praise your strength and justice to the skies,
tell of you who have worked such wonders.
O God, who is like you?

You have burdened me with bitter troubles
but you will give me back my life.
You will raise me from the depths of the earth;
you will exalt me and console me again.

So I will give you thanks on the lyre
for your faithful love, my God.
To you will I sing with the harp,
to you, the Holy One of Israel.
When I sing to you my lips shall rejoice
and my soul, which you have redeemed.

And all day long my tongue
shall tell the tale of your justice....

God of eternity,
you are my joy from my youth
and my hope in old age.
By your steadfast love you master the changing world
and dominate the flow of the centuries.
We implore you:
See our lives that flow like water through our fingers!
Help us to realize that only that time is lost
in which we forget to love you,
and that the only old age which threatens us
is that of our sins.
May we grow young again
each day of our lives
until that day comes when we will be young enough
to enter your eternal kingdom!

THE PROMISED KING

O God, give your judgment to the king,
to a king's son your justice,
that he may judge your people in justice
and your poor in right judgment.

May the mountains bring forth peace for the people
and the hills, justice.
May he defend the poor of the people
and save the children of the needy....

He shall endure like the sun and the moon
from age to age.
He shall descend like rain on the meadow,
like raindrops on the earth.

In his days justice shall flourish
and peace till the moon fails.
He shall rule from sea to sea,
from the Great River to earth's bounds.

Before him his enemies shall fall,
his foes lick the dust.
The kings of Tarshish and the seacoasts
shall pay him tribute.

The kings of Sheba and Seba
shall bring him gifts.
Before him all kings shall fall prostrate,
all nations shall serve him.

For he shall save the poor when they cry
and the needy who are helpless.
He will have pity on the weak
and save the lives of the poor.

From oppression he will rescue their lives,
to him their blood is dear.
Long may he live,
may the gold of Sheba be given him.
They shall pray for him without ceasing
and bless him all the day.

May corn be abundant in the land
to the peaks of the mountains.

JESUS, THE NEWBORN KING   *Matthew 2:1-2, 11*
When Jesus was born in Bethlehem of Judea, in the days of Herod the King, Wise
Men from the east arrived in Jerusalem. They said, "Where is the newborn king
of the Jews? We have seen his star in the east and have come to give him
homage."
Entering into the house, they saw the child with Mary his mother. They fell down
and gave him homage. Then, they opened their treasures and offered him gifts,
gold, frankincense, and myrrh.

May its fruit rustle like Lebanon;
may men flourish in the cities
like grass on the earth.

May his name be blessed forever
and endure like the sun.
Every tribe shall be blessed in him,
all nations bless his name.

Blessed be the Lord, God of Israel,
who alone works wonders,
ever blessed his glorious name.
Let his glory fill the earth.

Amen! Amen!

Blessed are you, God of Israel,
for your Son Jesus Christ!

He is the king of peace;
he defends the poor of the people;
he saves the children of the needy;
he rescues the weak from oppression.

May our lives proclaim his kingdom on earth
as it is in heaven!
May we help his justice to flourish
and his peace to reign from sea to sea!
May all people, like the kings of Sheba and Seba,
recognize the power of his love
and bless you forever and ever!

HOW LOVELY IS YOUR DWELLING PLACE

How lovely is your dwelling place,
Lord, God of hosts.

My soul is longing and yearning,
is yearning for the courts of the Lord.
My heart and my soul ring out their joy
to God, the living God.

The sparrow herself finds a home
and the swallow a nest for her brood;
she lays her young by your altars,
Lord of hosts, my king and my God.

They are happy, who dwell in your house,
forever singing your praise.
They are happy, whose strength is in you,
in whose hearts are the roads to Zion.

As they go through the Bitter Valley
they make it a place of springs,
the autumn rain covers it with blessings.
They walk with ever growing strength,
they will see the God of gods in Zion.

O Lord God of hosts, hear my prayer,
give ear, O God of Jacob.
Turn your eyes, O God, our shield,
look on the face of your anointed.

One day within your courts
is better than a thousand elsewhere.
The threshold of the house of God
I prefer to the dwellings of the wicked.

For the Lord God is a rampart, a shield;
he will give us his favor and glory.
The Lord will not refuse any good
to those who walk without blame.

Lord, God of hosts,
happy the man who trusts in you!

Even to the sparrow and swallow you give the joy of a home!
Give to us, who suffer on the road to heaven,
the joy of meeting you face-to-face,
in your holy dwelling place, on the day of your love.

JUSTICE AND PEACE EMBRACE

O Lord, you once favored your land
and revived the fortunes of Jacob,
you forgave the guilt of your people
and covered all their sins.
You averted all your rage,
you calmed the heat of your anger.

Revive us now, God, our helper!
Put an end to your grievance against us.
Will you be angry with us forever,
will your anger never cease?

Will you not restore again our life
that your people may rejoice in you?
Let us see, O Lord, your mercy
and give us your saving help.

I will hear what the Lord God has to say,
a voice that speaks of peace,
peace for his people and his friends
and those who turn to him in their hearts.
His help is near for those who fear him
and his glory will dwell in our land.

Mercy and faithfulness have met;
justice and peace have embraced.
Faithfulness shall spring from the earth
and justice look down from heaven.

The Lord will make us prosper
and our earth shall yield its fruit.
Justice shall march before him
and peace shall follow his steps.

God our Father,
in your Son Jesus Christ, the little child of Bethlehem,
mercy and faithfulness have met each other,
and justice and peace have kissed.
We pray you: Help us to live in such a way
that we may be to our brothers and sisters
the revelation of your mercy and faithfulness,
of your justice and peace on earth.

JESUS CHRIST, OUR PEACE   *Ephesians 2:14, 16*
He—Jesus Christ!—is our peace.... He reconciled us to God in one body through
his cross. In himself he killed hate.

PRAYER IN DISTRESS

Turn your ear, O Lord, and give answer
for I am poor and needy.
Preserve my life, for I am faithful:
save the servant who trusts in you.

You are my God, have mercy on me, Lord,
for I cry to you all the day long.
Give joy to your servant, O Lord,
for to you I lift up my soul.

O Lord, you are good and forgiving,
full of love to all who call.
Give heed, O Lord, to my prayer
and attend to the sound of my voice.

In the day of distress I will call
and surely you will reply.
Among the gods there is none like you, O Lord;
nor work to compare with yours.

All the nations shall come to adore you
and glorify your name, O Lord:
for you are great and do marvelous deeds,
you who alone are God.

Show me, Lord, your way
so that I may walk in your truth.
Guide my heart to fear your name.

I will praise you, Lord my God, with all my heart
and glorify your name forever;
for your love to me has been great:
you have saved me from the depths of the grave.

The proud have risen against me;
ruthless men seek my life:
to you they pay no heed.

But you, God of mercy and compassion,
slow to anger, O Lord,
abounding in love and truth,
turn and take pity on me.

O give your strength to your servant
and save your handmaid's son.
Show me a sign of your favor....

HYMN TO GOD'S FAITHFULNESS

I will sing forever of your love, O Lord;
through all ages my mouth will proclaim your truth.
Of this I am sure, that your love lasts forever,
that your truth is firmly established as the heavens.

"With my chosen one I have made a covenant;
I have sworn to David my servant:
I will establish your dynasty forever
and set up your throne through all ages."

The heavens proclaim your wonders, O Lord;
the assembly of your holy ones proclaims your truth.
For who in the skies can compare with the Lord
or who is like the Lord among the sons of God?

A God to be feared in the council of the holy ones,
great and dreadful to all around him.
O Lord God of hosts, who is your equal?
You are mighty, O Lord, and truth is your garment.

It is you who rule the sea in its pride;
it is you who still the surging of its waves.
It is you who trod Rahab underfoot like a corpse,
scattering your foes with your mighty arm.

The heavens are yours, the world is yours.
It is you who founded the earth and all it holds;
it is you who created the North and the South.
Tabor and Hermon shout with joy at your name.

Yours is a mighty arm, O Lord;
your hand is strong, your right hand ready.
Justice and right are the pillars of your throne,
love and truth walk in your presence.

Happy the people who acclaim such a king,
who walk, O Lord, in the light of your face,
who find their joy every day in your name,
who make your justice the source of their bliss.

For you, O Lord, are the glory of their strength;
by your favor it is that our might is exalted:
for our ruler is in the keeping of the Lord;
our king in the keeping of the Holy One of Israel....

Jesus, Son of David, have mercy on us!   *Mt 20:30*
And we will sing your love through eternity.

UNDER THE DIVINE WINGS

He who dwells in the shelter of the Most High
and abides in the shade of the Almighty
says to the Lord: "My refuge,
my stronghold, my God in whom I trust!"

It is he who will free you from the snare
of the fowler who seeks to destroy you;
he will conceal you with his pinions
and under his wings you will find refuge.

You will not fear the terror of the night
nor the arrow that flies by day,
nor the plague that prowls in the darkness
nor the scourge that lays waste at noon.

A thousand may fall at your side,
ten thousand fall at your right,
you, it will never approach;
his faithfulness is buckler and shield.

Your eyes have only to look
to see how the wicked are repaid,
you who have said: "Lord, my refuge!"
and have made the Most High your dwelling.

Upon you no evil shall fall,
no plague approach where you dwell.
For you has he commanded his angels,
to keep you in all your ways.

They shall bear you upon their hands
lest you strike your foot against a stone.
On the lion and the viper you will tread
and trample the young lion and the dragon.

Since he clings to me in love, I will free him;
protect him for he knows my name.
When he calls I shall answer: "I am with you."
I will save him in distress and give him glory.

With length of life I will content him;
I shall let him see my saving power.*

JESUS IN PSALM 91   *Matthew 4:1...11*
Jesus was led up into the desert by the Spirit to be tempted by the devil.... The
devil took him to the holy city and set him on the pinnacle of the temple, and said
to him, "If you are the Son of God, throw yourself down; for it is written:

To his angels he will give charge of you,
and: *Upon their hands they will bear you up*
lest you dash your foot against a stone."

Jesus replied, "It is written also 'you shall not tempt the Lord your God.'" ...
Then the devil left him, and behold, angels came and ministered to him.

*See the prayer, "I Will Answer Him Who Calls upon Me," p. 151.

THE SONG OF THE JUST

It is good to give thanks to the Lord
to make music to your name, O Most High,
to proclaim your love in the morning
and your truth in the watches of the night,
on the ten-stringed lyre and the lute,
with the murmuring sound of the harp.

Your deeds, O Lord, have made me glad;
for the work of your hands I shout with joy.
O Lord, how great are your works!
How deep are your designs!...

The just will flourish like the palm tree
and grow like a Lebanon cedar.

Planted in the house of the Lord
they will flourish in the courts of our God,
still bearing fruit when they are old,
still full of sap, still green,
to proclaim that the Lord is just;
in him, my rock, there is no wrong.

How good it is for us to sing your holy name,
Lord Jesus Christ, God of kindness!
Plant us in your paradise!
In the morning, at noontime, in the evening of our life,
may we bear fruit for the glory of your Father!

TODAY LISTEN TO HIS VOICE

Come, ring out our joy to the Lord;
hail the rock who saves us.
Let us come before him, giving thanks,
with songs let us hail the Lord.

A mighty God is the Lord,
a great king above all gods.
In his hand are the depths of the earth;
the heights of the mountains are his.
To him belongs the sea, for he made it
and the dry land shaped by his hands.

Come in; let us bow and bend low;
let us kneel before the God who made us
for he is our God and we
the people who belong to his pasture,
the flock that is led by his hand.

O that today you would listen to his voice!
"Harden not your hearts as at Meribah,
as on that day at Massah in the desert
when your fathers put me to test;
when they tried me, though they saw my work...."

Blessed are you, Lord our God,
who calls us into your presence
and gives us the joy of worshiping you!
Grant us the grace, we implore you,
to listen to your voice today
and never to harden our hearts.
We are your people, be our Father,
forever and ever!

JESUS CHRIST IN PSALM 95   *Hebrews 3:6...14*

Christ was faithful over God's house as a son. And we are his house as long as we
hold fast the confidence and the glory of our hope. Therefore, as the Holy Spirit
says:

> *Today, if you hear his voice,*
> *harden not your hearts....*

Take care, brethren, that there is not anyone among you with a bad, unbelieving
heart, leading you away from the living God. But exhort one another every day,
as long as this "today" lasts, so that none of you may be hardened by the lure of
the sin. For we share in Christ, if we hold fast our confidence from the beginning
till the end.

SING TO THE LORD A NEW SONG

O sing a new song to the Lord,
sing to the Lord all the earth.
O sing to the Lord, bless his name.

Proclaim his help day by day,
tell among the nations his glory
and his wonders among all the peoples.

The Lord is great and worthy of praise,
to be feared above all gods;
the gods of the heathens are naught.

It was the Lord who made the heavens,
his are majesty and state and power
and splendor in his holy place.

Give the Lord, you families of peoples,
give the Lord glory and power,
give the Lord the glory of his name.

Bring an offering and enter his courts,
worship the Lord in his temple.
O earth, tremble before him.

Proclaim to the nations: "God is king."
The world he made firm in its place;
he will judge the peoples in fairness.

Let the heavens rejoice and earth be glad,
let the sea and all within it thunder praise,
let the land and all it bears rejoice,
all the trees of the wood shout for joy

at the presence of the Lord for he comes,
he comes to rule the earth.
With justice he will rule the world,
he will judge the peoples with his truth.

A new song was heard on our earth
when the angels of Bethlehem sang:
"Glory to God in the highest!"
Come, Lord, rule the world in justice
and give peace to all who enjoy your love.

THE KINDNESS OF GOD ON EARTH   *Titus 2:11; 3:4-5*
The grace of God has appeared for the salvation of all men.
When the goodness and the kindness of God our Savior appeared, he saved us,
not because of any righteous deeds we had done, but because of his own mercy.

SHOUT TO THE LORD, ALL THE EARTH

Sing a new song to the Lord
for he has worked wonders.
His right hand and his holy arm
have brought salvation.

The Lord has made known his salvation;
has shown his justice to the nations.
He has remembered his truth and love
for the house of Israel.

All the ends of the earth have seen
the salvation of our God.
Shout to the Lord all the earth,
ring out your joy.

Sing psalms to the Lord with the harp,
with the sound of music.
With trumpets and the sound of the horn
acclaim the King, the Lord.

Let the sea and all within it thunder;
the world, and all its peoples.
Let the rivers clap their hands
and the hills ring out their joy

at the presence of the Lord: for he comes,
he comes to rule the earth.
He will rule the world with justice
and the peoples with fairness.

God, our heavenly Father,
you remembered your truth and your love
when you gave us your Son Jesus Christ,
born of the Virgin Mary.
Help us sing your praise,
not only with harps, trumpets, and melodious songs,
but, above all, with holy and joyful lives.
Each day may our new song
be our greater love for our brothers and sisters,
through Jesus Christ, your Son and our brother,
forever and ever.

REJOICE! THE LORD IS NEAR   *Philippians 4:4...7*
Rejoice in the Lord always! I say it again. Rejoice!...The Lord is near. In nothing
be anxious, but in everything, by prayer and supplication, with thanksgiving,
let your requests be known before God. And the peace of God, which surpasses all
understanding, will keep your hearts and your minds in Christ Jesus.

ENTER HIS COURTS WITH SONGS OF PRAISE

Cry out with joy to the Lord, all the earth.
Serve the Lord with gladness.
Come before him, singing for joy.

Know that he, the Lord, is God.
He made us, we belong to him,
we are his people, the sheep of his flock.

Go within his gates, giving thanks.
Enter his courts with songs of praise.
Give thanks to him and bless his name.

Indeed, how good is the Lord,
eternal his merciful love.
He is faithful from age to age.

Blessed are you, God our Father!

Your love has gathered us together
to stand in your presence
and serve you with gladness.

Let us go within your gates of thanksgiving,
let us enter your courts of joy.

While we celebrate your love,
please recognize in our songs
the voice of your Son Jesus Christ,
our Savior and our brother,
forever and ever.

YOU CAME NEAR TO THE FEAST OF HEAVEN   *Hebrews 12:22-24*
You came near to Mount Zion, to the city of the living God, to the heavenly
Jerusalem, to the myriads of angels in festal gathering, to the assembly of the
firstborn [angels] enrolled in heaven, to a judge who is God of all, to the spirits of
just men made perfect, to Jesus, the mediator of the New Covenant.

GOD IS LOVE

My soul, give thanks to the Lord,
all my being, bless his holy name.
My soul, give thanks to the Lord
and never forget all his blessings.

It is he who forgives all your guilt,
who heals every one of your ills,
who redeems your life from the grave,
who crowns you with love and compassion,
who fills your life with good things,
renewing your youth like an eagle's.

The Lord does deeds of justice,
gives judgment for all who are oppressed.
He made known his ways to Moses
and his deeds to Israel's sons.

The Lord is compassion and love,
slow to anger and rich in mercy.
His wrath will come to an end;
he will not be angry forever.
He does not treat us according to our sins
nor repay us according to our faults.

For as the heavens are high above the earth
so strong is his love for those who fear him.
As far as the east is from the west
so far does he remove our sins.

As a father has compassion on his sons,
the Lord has pity on those who fear him;
for he knows of what we are made,
he remembers that we are dust.

As for man, his days are like grass;
he flowers like the flower of the field;
the wind blows and he is gone
and his place never sees him again.

But the love of the Lord is everlasting
upon those who hold him in fear;
his justice reaches out to children's children
when they keep his covenant in truth,
when they keep his will in their mind.

The Lord has set his sway in heaven
and his kingdom is ruling over all.

GOD IS LOVE   *1 John 4:16-17*
As for us, we know and we believe the love God has for us. God is love, and he who
abides in love abides in God, and God abides in him. In this, the love of God is
made perfect with us, that we may have confidence for the day of judgment,
because as he is, so are we in this world.

Give thanks to the Lord, all his angels,
mighty in power, fulfilling his word,
who heed the voice of his word.

Give thanks to the Lord, all his hosts,
his servants who do his will.
Give thanks to the Lord, all his works,
in every place where he rules.
My soul, give thanks to the Lord!

Blessed are you, Lord our God,
God full of mercy and compassion,
because you created us
and gave us the joy of faith
so we may see
how marvelous is your kindness,
how gracious and infinite is your pardon!

See our lowliness and humbleness.
We are dust of the earth.
But you are the heaven of kindness!
Our days pass away like grass,
like flowers of the field that bloom and fade;
the empty wind sweeps us away.
But you are the eternity of mercy!

We thank you for being
our God and Father
in Jesus Christ and in the Spirit of love!

SPLENDOR OF CREATION

Bless the Lord, my soul!
Lord God, how great you are,
clothed in majesty and glory,
wrapped in light as in a robe!

You stretch out the heavens like a tent.
Above the rains you build your dwelling.
You make the clouds your chariot,
you walk on the wings of the wind,
you make the winds your messengers
and flashing fire your servants.

You founded the earth on its base,
to stand firm from age to age.
You wrapped it with the ocean like a cloak:
the waters stood higher than the mountains.

At your threat they took to flight;
at the voice of your thunder they fled.
They rose over the mountains and flowed down
to the place which you had appointed.
You set limits they might not pass
lest they return to cover the earth.

You make springs gush forth in the valleys:
they flow in between the hills.
They give drink to all the beasts of the field;
the wild asses quench their thirst.
On their banks dwell the birds of heaven;
from the branches they sing their song.

From your dwelling you water the hills;
earth drinks its fill of your gift.
You make the grass grow for the cattle
and the plants to serve man's needs,

that he may bring forth bread from the earth
and wine to cheer man's heart;
oil to make his face shine
and bread to strengthen man's heart.

The trees of the Lord drink their fill,
the cedars he planted on Lebanon;
there the birds build their nests:
on the treetop the stork has her home.
The goats find a home on the mountains
and rabbits hide in the rocks.

You made the moon to mark the months;
the sun knows the time for its setting.
When you spread the darkness it is night
and all the beasts of the forest creep forth.

The young lions roar for their prey
and ask their food from God.

At the rising of the sun they steal away
and go to rest in their dens.
Man goes forth to his work,
to labor till evening falls.

How many are your works, O Lord!
In wisdom you have made them all.
The earth is full of your riches.

There is the sea, vast and wide,
with its moving swarms past counting,
living things great and small.
The ships are moving there
and the monsters you made to play with.

All of these look to you
to give them their food in due season.
You give it, they gather it up:
you open your hand, they have their fill.

You hide your face, they are dismayed;
you take back your spirit, they die,
returning to the dust from which they came.
You send forth your spirit, they are created;
and you renew the face of the earth.

May the glory of the Lord last forever!
May the Lord rejoice in his works!...

I will sing to the Lord all my life,
make music to my God while I live....

Bless the Lord, my soul.

We bless you, O God, Father of Jesus Christ,
the firstborn of all creation and the fountain of all splendor!
Your Spirit renews the face of the earth;
may it also renew the depths of our hearts!

THE MESSIAH, KING, PRIEST, AND JUDGE

The Lord's revelation to my Master:
   "Sit on my right:
Your foes I will put beneath your feet."

The Lord will wield from Zion
   your scepter of power:
rule in the midst of all your foes.

A prince from the day of your birth
   on the holy mountains;
from the womb before the dawn I begot you.

The Lord has sworn an oath he will not change.
   "You are a priest forever,
a priest like Melchizedek of old."

The Master standing at your right hand
will shatter kings in the day of his great wrath....

He shall drink from the stream by the wayside
and therefore he shall lift up his head.

Jesus!
Messiah sent by your Father,
King of kings and Lord of lords,
Priest of the new and eternal Covenant,
Judge of the living and the dead,
Offspring of David and bright Morning Star,   *Rv 22:16*
Jesus! My love and my all!

JESUS CHRIST IN PSALM 110   *Mark 12:35-37*
As Jesus was teaching in the temple, he said, "How can the scribes say that the
Messiah is David's son? David himself, inspired by the Holy Spirit, declared:

The Lord said to my Lord:
'Sit at my right hand
until I make your enemies your footstool.'

David himself calls him 'Lord,' so, how is he his son?" And so the large crowd
heard him gladly.

Romans 8:34-35
Christ Jesus died; he was raised from the dead; he *is at the right hand* of God; he
intercedes for us. Who shall separate us from the love of Christ?

HE SENDS DELIVERANCE TO HIS PEOPLE

I will thank the Lord with all my heart
in the meeting of the just and their assembly.
Great are the works of the Lord;
to be pondered by all who love them.

Majestic and glorious his work,
his justice stands firm forever.
He makes us remember his wonders.
The Lord is compassion and love.

He gives food to those who fear him;
keeps his covenant ever in mind.
He has shown his might to his people
by giving them the lands of the nations.

His works are justice and truth:
his precepts are all of them sure,
standing firm forever and ever:
they are made in uprightness and truth.

He has sent deliverance to his people
and established his covenant forever.
Holy his name, to be feared.

To fear the Lord is the beginning of wisdom;
all who do so prove themselves wise.
His praise shall last forever!

Blessed are you, God our Father,
gracious and merciful Lord!

Send your deliverance to your people,
your Son Jesus Christ,
our Savior and our brother,
forever and ever.

JESUS, OUR FREEDOM   *John 8:31-32, 36*
Jesus said, "If you keep my word, you are truly my disciples. You will know the
truth, and the truth will set you free....If the Son makes you free, you will be
really free."

AS A LIGHT IN THE DARKNESS

Happy the man who fears the Lord,
who takes delight in all his commands.
His sons will be powerful on earth;
the children of the upright are blessed.

Riches and wealth are in his house;
his justice stands firm forever.
He is a light in the darkness for the upright:
he is generous, merciful and just.

The good man takes pity and lends,
he conducts his affairs with honor.
The just man will never waver:
he will be remembered forever.

He has no fear of evil news;
with a firm heart he trusts in the Lord.
With a steadfast heart he will not fear;
he will see the downfall of his foes.

Openhanded, he gives to the poor;
his justice stands firm forever.
His head will be raised in glory.

The wicked man sees and is angry,
grinds his teeth and fades away;
the desire of the wicked leads to doom.

Glow through the darkness of our hearts;
be a light of love for your people,
gracious and merciful Lord,
Jesus Christ!

THE MORNING STAR IN OUR HEARTS   *2 Peter 1:19*
We have the prophetic Word. You do well to pay attention to it, as a light shining
in the darkness, until the day dawns and the morning star rises in our hearts.

TO THE GOD OF GLORY AND MERCY

Praise, O servants of the Lord,
praise the name of the Lord!
May the name of the Lord be blessed
both now and forevermore!
From the rising of the sun to its setting
praised be the name of the Lord!

High above all nations is the Lord,
above the heavens his glory.
Who is like the Lord, our God,
who has risen on high to his throne
yet stoops from the heights to look down,
to look down upon heaven and earth?

From the dust he lifts up the lowly,
from the dungheap he raises the poor
to set him in the company of princes,
yes, with the princes of his people.
To the childless wife he gives a home
and gladdens her heart with children.

Who is there like you,
O God of all marvels
and creator of all joys?
From the dust of the dead
you raised up your Son Jesus Christ.
From the dungheap of their sins
you pull back those who love you.
You have made your Church
a happy mother in the midst of her children.
Yes, blessed is your name, Lord our God,
through Jesus Christ, your Son,
both now and forever.

MY SOUL MAGNIFIES THE LORD   *Luke 1:46...52*
Mary said, "My soul magnifies the Lord and my spirit rejoices in God my Savior.
For he has looked upon the lowliness of his servant.... His mercy is from age to
age on those who fear him.... He has put down the mighty from their thrones; he
has raised the lowly."

I LOVE THE LORD

I love the Lord for he has heard
the cry of my appeal;
for he turned his ear to me
in the day when I called him.

They surrounded me, the snares of death,
with the anguish of the tomb;
they caught me, sorrow and distress.
I called on the Lord's name.

O Lord my God, deliver me!

How gracious is the Lord, and just;
our God has compassion.
The Lord protects the simple hearts;
I was helpless so he saved me.

Turn back, my soul, to your rest
for the Lord has been good;
he has kept my soul from death,
my eyes from tears
and my feet from stumbling.

I will walk in the presence of the Lord
in the land of the living.

I trusted, even when I said:
"I am sorely afflicted,"
and when I said in my alarm:
"No man can be trusted."

How can I repay the Lord
for his goodness to me?
The cup of salvation I will raise;
I will call on the Lord's name.

My vows to the Lord I will fulfill
before all his people.
O precious in the eyes of the Lord
is the death of his faithful.

Your servant, Lord, your servant am I;
you have loosened my bonds.
A thanksgiving sacrifice I make:
I will call on the Lord's name.

THE CUP OF BLESSING   *1 Corinthians 10:16-17*
The cup of blessing which we bless, is it not participation in the blood of Christ?
The bread which we break, is it not participation in the body of Christ? There is
one bread; we, many though we are, form one body, for we all partake of this one
bread.

My vows to the Lord I will fulfill
before all his people,
in the courts of the house of the Lord,
in your midst, O Jerusalem.

Gracious Lord and merciful God,
when the strings of sins encompassed me
and the snares of sadness seized upon me,
you saved me by your love,
through the resurrection of Christ.
You have made me walk in the land of the living.

How shall I return your kindness?
Accept the sacrifice of thanksgiving
of your Son Jesus Christ,
our Savior and brother forever and ever.

PSALM 117

DOXOLOGY OF ALL THE NATIONS

O praise the Lord, all you nations,
acclaim him all you peoples!

Strong is his love for us;
he is faithful forever.

Lord Jesus Christ,
we carry your name,
we sing your praise.
Give us the grace, we beg you,
to be the sign of your love
among all the nations.

MAKE DISCIPLES OF ALL THE NATIONS   *Matthew 28:18...20*
"All authority has been given to me in heaven and on earth. Go, therefore, and
make disciples of all the nations.... And behold, I am with you always, to the
close of the age."

THIS IS THE DAY THE LORD HAS MADE

Give thanks to the Lord for he is good,
for his love endures forever.

Let the sons of Israel say:
"His love endures forever."
Let the sons of Aaron say:
"His love endures forever."
Let those who fear the Lord say:
"His love endures forever."

I called to the Lord in my distress;
he answered and freed me.
The Lord is at my side; I do not fear.
What can man do against me?
The Lord is at my side as my helper:
I shall look down on my foes.

It is better to take refuge in the Lord
than to trust in men:
it is better to take refuge in the Lord
than to trust in princes....

I was thrust down, thrust down and falling
but the Lord was my helper.
The Lord is my strength and my song;
he was my savior.
There are shouts of joy and victory
in the tents of the just.

The Lord's right hand has triumphed;
his right hand raised me.

JESUS IN PSALM 118   *Matthew 21:1...11, 42-43*
When they were near to Jerusalem and came in sight of Bethphage on the Mount
of Olives,... the crowds of people spread their cloaks on the road, while others cut
branches from the trees and spread them on the road. And the crowds that went
before him and that followed him, were all shouting:

Hosanna to the Son of David!
Blessed is he who comes in the name of the Lord!
Hosanna in the highest!

When he entered Jerusalem, the whole city was stirred, asking, "Who is this?"
And the crowds answered, "This is the prophet Jesus from Nazareth in
Galilee."...
Jesus said [to the Pharisees]: "Have you never read in the Scriptures:

The very stone which the builders rejected
has become the cornerstone.
This is the work of the Lord, a marvel in our eyes?

Therefore I tell you, the kingdom of God will be taken away from you and given
to a people who will produce its fruit."

The Lord's right hand has triumphed;
I shall not die, I shall live
and recount his deeds.
I was punished, I was punished by the Lord,
but not doomed to die.

Open to me the gates of holiness:
I will enter and give thanks.
This is the Lord's own gate
where the just may enter.
I will thank you for you have answered
and you are my savior.

The stone which the builders rejected
has become the cornerstone.
This is the work of the Lord,
a marvel in our eyes.
This day was made by the Lord;
we rejoice and are glad.

O Lord, grant us salvation;
O Lord, grant success.
Blessed in the name of the Lord
is he who comes.
We bless you from the house of the Lord;
the Lord God is our light.

Go forward in procession with branches
even to the altar.
You are my God, I thank you.
My God, I praise you.
Give thanks to the Lord for he is good;
for his love endures forever.

Jesus Lord!
Jesus, cornerstone of the joy of the world,
Jesus, gate opened in the temple of heaven,
Jesus, blessed one who came in the name of your Father,
Jesus, joyful shout of victory over death,
Jesus, my strength and my courage in fear!

Jesus, blessed are you for the day of your resurrection!
Blessed are you for the day you will come again!
Then I will sing your love forever and ever.

GUARD OUR GOING AND OUR COMING

I lift up my eyes to the mountains:
from where shall come my help?
My help shall come from the Lord
who made heaven and earth.

May he never allow you to stumble!
Let him sleep not, your guard.
No, he sleeps not nor slumbers,
Israel's guard.

The Lord is your guard and your shade;
at your right side he stands.
By day the sun shall not smite you
nor the moon in the night.

The Lord will guard you from evil,
he will guard your soul.
The Lord will guard your going and coming
both now and forever.

Father of Jesus and Source of the Spirit,
we came forth from your heart
when we were born in this world.
We return to you
when we show you our love on the pilgrimage of this life.
Watch over our going and our coming to you,
through Jesus Christ, in the Spirit of love.

PSALM 122

LET US GO TO GOD'S HOUSE

I rejoiced when I heard them say:
"Let us go to God's house."
And now our feet are standing
within your gates, O Jerusalem.

Jerusalem is built as a city
strongly compact.
It is there that the tribes go up,
the tribes of the Lord.

For Israel's law it is,
there to praise the Lord's name.

IN MY FATHER'S HOUSE   *Luke 2:41-42, 49*
The parents of Jesus went up to Jerusalem every year at the feast of the Passover.
When he was twelve years old, they went up according to the custom.... Jesus
said, "I must be in my Father's house!"

There were set the thrones of judgment
of the house of David.

For the peace of Jerusalem pray:
"Peace be to your homes!
May peace reign in your walls,
in your palaces, peace!"

For love of my brethren and friends
I say: "Peace upon you!"
For love of the house of the Lord
I will ask for your good.

What a joy it will be for us, Lord,
one day to enter the dwelling
that your love has created for us,
to take the place that you have prepared for us,
and to give you thanks with all our brothers and sisters
in an eternity of happiness!

PSALM 123

TO YOU I LIFT UP MY EYES

To you have I lifted up my eyes,
you who dwell in the heavens:
my eyes, like the eyes of slaves
on the hand of their lords.

Like the eyes of a servant
on the hand of her mistress,
so our eyes are on the Lord our God
till he show us his mercy.

Have mercy on us, Lord, have mercy.
We are filled with contempt.
Indeed all too full is our soul
with the scorn of the rich,
with the proud man's disdain.

To you, our Father in heaven,
we lift up our eyes.
We ask for nothing
but that you see us
as the children of your handmaid, the Virgin Mary,
and the brothers and sisters of her Son, Jesus Christ.

LIGHT IN THE EYES OF OUR HEARTS   *Ephesians 1:17-18*
May the Father of glory ... enlighten the eyes of your hearts, that you may know
the hope to which he has called you.

SONG OF THE RETURN

When the Lord delivered Zion from bondage,
it seemed like a dream.
Then was our mouth filled with laughter,
on our lips there were songs.

The heathens themselves said: "What marvels
the Lord worked for them!"
What marvels the Lord worked for us!
Indeed we were glad.

Deliver us, O Lord, from our bondage
as streams in dry land.
Those who are sowing in tears
will sing when they reap.

They go out, they go out, full of tears,
carrying seed for the sowing:
they come back, they come back, full of song,
carrying their sheaves.

Lord Jesus,
with the tears of your agony
you have sown the seeds of our joy.
You have planted them in the soil of our hearts;
make them bear much fruit!
Then may we celebrate your wonders
by singing with Mary, your Mother,
"The Lord has done great things for us,
holy is his name!"

JESUS, THE GRAIN IN THE EARTH   *John 12:24*
"Amen, amen, I say to you, unless the grain of wheat falls in the earth and dies, it
remains alone; but if it dies, it bears fruit."

IF THE LORD DOES NOT BUILD THE HOUSE

If the Lord does not build the house,
in vain do its builders labor;
if the Lord does not watch over the city,
in vain does the watchman keep vigil.

In vain is your earlier rising,
your going later to rest,
you who toil for the bread you eat:
when he pours gifts on his beloved while they slumber.

Truly sons are a gift from the Lord,
a blessing, the fruit of the womb.
Indeed the sons of youth
are like arrows in the hand of a warrior.

O the happiness of the man
who has filled his quiver with these arrows!
He will have no cause for shame
when he disputes with his foes in the gateways.

God our Father,
creator of your heaven
and builder of our earth,
we pray to you:
Build for yourself the house of your Church,
founding it on the Word.
Build also for us a home to live in,
rooting it in love,
you who have filled us with joy
in your beloved Jesus Christ.
He slept in death on the cross;
he rose in the light of resurrection.
To him be glory through all the ages.

THE HOUSE BUILT ON ROCK   *Matthew 7:24-25*
"Anyone who hears these words of mine and puts them in practice is like a wise
man who built his house on rock. The rain fell; the floods came; the storms blew
and beat upon that house. It did not collapse; it had been founded on rock."

MAY THE LORD BLESS YOU

O blessed are those who fear the Lord
and walk in his ways!

By the labor of your hands you shall eat.
You will be happy and prosper;
your wife like a fruitful vine
in the heart of your house;
your children like shoots of the olive,
around your table.

Indeed thus shall be blessed
the man who fears the Lord.
May the Lord bless you from Zion
all the days of your life!

May you see your children's children
in a happy Jerusalem! On Israel, peace!

Blessed are you, God our Father!
Blessed are you for husband and wife,
united in your love!
Blessed are you for the children, springing from their love!
Blessed are you for Mother Church,
gathering all your children in your heavenly home
for the eternal feast of your tenderness!

PSALM 130

OUT OF THE DEPTHS

Out of the depths I cry to you, O Lord,
Lord, hear my voice!
O let your ears be attentive
to the voice of my pleading.

If you, O Lord, should mark our guilt,
Lord, who would survive?
But with you is found forgiveness:
for this we revere you.

My soul is waiting for the Lord,
I count on his word.
My soul is longing for the Lord
more than watchman for daybreak.

TO SAVE WHAT WAS LOST   *Luke 19:10*
"The Son of Man came to seek and to save what was lost."

Let the watchman count on daybreak
and Israel on the Lord.

Because with the Lord there is mercy
and fullness of redemption,
Israel indeed he will redeem
from all its iniquity.

Only you, O Lord, know our hearts,
only you can give them the peace of pardon.
In the depths of our darkness,
more than the watchman longs for daybreak,
we long for the dawn of our salvation,
your kindness and your mercy in Jesus Christ.

PSALM 131

LIKE A CHILD

O Lord, my heart is not proud
nor haughty my eyes.
I have not gone after things too great
nor marvels beyond me.

Truly I have set my soul
in silence and peace.
A weaned child on its mother's breast,
even so is my soul.

O Israel, hope in the Lord
both now and forever.

We pray to you, Lord our Father.
As children, we trust in you.
As a Father, give us your love
in Jesus Christ, forever and ever.

LIKE CHILDREN　　　　　　　　　　　　　　　*Matthew 18:3-4*
"Amen, I say to you, unless you change and become like children, you will not
enter the kingdom of heaven. Whoever humbles himself like this child, he is the
greatest in the kingdom of heaven."

NOCTURNE

O come, bless the Lord,
all you who serve the Lord,
who stand in the house of the Lord,
in the courts of the house of our God.

Lift up your hands to the holy place
and bless the Lord through the night.
May the Lord bless you from Zion,
he who made both heaven and earth.

May our prayer in the night
reach your heart, God our Father,
whose home is in unapproachable light.
And may your everlasting blessing
illuminate the darkness of our hearts,
through Jesus Christ, the light of our lives,
forever and ever.

PSALM 136

GREAT LITANY OF THANKSGIVING

O give thanks to the Lord for he is good,
for his love endures forever.
Give thanks to the God of gods,
for his love endures forever.
Give thanks to the Lord of lords,
for his love endures forever;

who alone has wrought marvelous works,
for his love endures forever;
whose wisdom it was made the skies,
for his love endures forever;
who fixed the earth firmly on the seas,
for his love endures forever.

It was he who made the great lights,
for his love endures forever,

CHRIST'S SONG OF PASSOVER   *Matthew 26:19, 26-28, 30*
The disciples did as Jesus directed them and prepared the Passover.
As they were eating, Jesus took bread, said the blessing, broke it, and gave it to
his disciples, saying, "This is my body." Then he took a cup, gave thanks, and
gave it to them saying, "Drink of it, all of you; for this is my blood of the covenant,
which is poured out for many for the forgiveness of sins...." Then they sang a
hymn and went to the Mount of Olives.

the sun to rule in the day,
for his love endures forever,
the moon and stars in the night,
for his love endures forever....

He divided the Red Sea in two,
for his love endures forever;
he made Israel pass through the midst,
for his love endures forever;
he flung Pharaoh and his force in the sea,
for his love endures forever.

Through the desert his people he led,
for his love endures forever.
Nations in their greatness he struck,
for his love endures forever.
Kings in their splendor he slew,
for his love endures forever....

He let Israel inherit their land,
for his love endures forever.
On his servant their land he bestowed,
for his love endures forever.
He remembered us in our distress,
for his love endures forever.

And he snatched us away from our foes,
for his love endures forever.
He gives food to all living things,
for his love endures forever.
To the God of heaven give thanks,
for his love endures forever.

We bless you, Lord Jesus,
who sang this paschal psalm
with the apostles at the Last Supper!
To you we offer the songs of our lips and our hearts.
With our lips, we continue to sing to your Father.
With our hearts, we continue to love him.
In every circumstance of our life and even in death,
when we shall pass from the servitude of earth
to the liberty of the true Promised Land,
may we take up your refrain:
"His love endures forever!"

BY THE RIVERS OF BABYLON

By the rivers of Babylon
there we sat and wept,
remembering Zion;
on the poplars that grew there
we hung up our harps.

For it was there that they asked us,
our captors, for songs,
our oppressors, for joy.
"Sing to us," they said,
"one of Zion's songs."

O how could we sing
the song of the Lord
on alien soil?
If I forget you, Jerusalem,
let my right hand wither!

O let my tongue
cleave to my mouth
if I remember you not,
if I prize not Jerusalem
above all my joys!...

Our Father in heaven,
help us to realize
that we have no lasting dwelling here below,
but that we must seek after the city that is to come.
Teach us, also, to love this earth
in such a way that we never prefer it to heaven,
where you have prepared a place for us,
with your Son Jesus and the Spirit of love,
forever and ever.

THE CITY OF HEAVEN   *Hebrews 11:10; 13:14*
Abraham was looking forward to the city with foundations, whose builder is
God.... We have here no lasting city, but we seek ardently the city which is to
come.

OUR CITIZENSHIP IS IN HEAVEN   *Philippians 3:20-21*
Our citizenship is in heaven. From it we await a Savior, the Lord Jesus Christ. He
will change our lowly body to be like his glorious body.

IN THE PRESENCE OF THE ANGELS

I thank you, Lord, with all my heart,
you have heard the words of my mouth.
In the presence of the angels I will bless you.
I will adore before your holy temple.

I thank you for your faithfulness and love
which excel all we ever knew of you.
On the day I called, you answered;
you increased the strength of my soul.

All earth's kings shall thank you
when they hear the words of your mouth.
They shall sing of the Lord's ways:
"How great is the glory of the Lord!"

The Lord is high yet he looks on the lowly
and the haughty he knows from afar.
Though I walk in the midst of affliction
you give me life and frustrate my foes.

You stretch out your hand and save me,
your hand will do all things for me.
Your love, O Lord, is eternal,
discard not the work of your hands.

O Lord, when we gather in your presence to worship you,
we meet the angels of heaven
who always stand before your face.
With them, and the saints of all ages,
we form one family,
the family of all those who love you!

Listen, then, to the prayer of that family,
as with one voice we acclaim you:
Your love, our Lord and Father, is eternal,
through Jesus Christ, in the Holy Spirit,
forever and ever.

THE GOLDEN BOWLS OF INCENSE   *Revelation 5:8-9*
The four living creatures and the twenty-four elders [angels] fell down before the
Lamb. Each one of them was holding a harp and had a golden bowl of incense,
which are the prayers of the saints. They sang a new song.

THE ALL-KNOWING AND EVER-PRESENT GOD

O Lord, you search me and you know me,
you know my resting and my rising,
you discern my purpose from afar.
You mark when I walk or lie down,
all my ways lie open to you.

Before ever a word is on my tongue
you know it, O Lord, through and through.
Behind and before you besiege me,
your hand ever laid upon me.
Too wonderful for me, this knowledge,
too high, beyond my reach.

O where can I go from your spirit,
or where can I flee from your face?
If I climb the heavens, you are there.
If I lie in the grave, you are there.

If I take the wings of the dawn
and dwell at the sea's furthest end,
even there your hand would lead me,
your right hand would hold me fast.

If I say: "Let the darkness hide me
and the light around me be night,"
even darkness is not dark for you
and the night is as clear as the day.

For it was you who created my being,
knit me together in my mother's womb.
I thank you for the wonder of my being,
for the wonders of all your creation.

Already you knew my soul,
my body held no secret from you
when I was being fashioned in secret
and molded in the depths of the earth.

Your eyes saw all my actions,
they were all of them written in your book;
every one of my days was decreed
before one of them came into being.

To me, how mysterious your thoughts,
the sum of them not to be numbered!
If I count them, they are more than the sand;
to finish, I must be eternal, like you....

O THE DEPTH OF GOD'S WISDOM!   *Romans 11:33, 36*
O the depth of the riches and wisdom and knowledge of God! How unsearchable
his judgments, how inscrutable his ways!... From him, through him, and to him
are all things. To him be the glory forever!

O search me, God, and know my heart.
O test me and know my thoughts.
See that I follow not the wrong path
and lead me in the path of life eternal.

Lord, you know me, and your hand rests upon me!
My day and my night are light before you!
You knit me together in my mother's womb.
Lord, you know everything.
You know that I love you.
Keep me in your hand!

PSALM 145

THE LORD IS KIND AND FULL OF COMPASSION

I will give you glory, O God my King,
I will bless your name forever.

I will bless you day after day
and praise your name forever.
The Lord is great, highly to be praised,
his greatness cannot be measured.

Age to age shall proclaim your works,
shall declare your mighty deeds,
shall speak of your splendor and glory,
tell the tale of your wonderful works.
They will speak of your terrible deeds,
recount your greatness and might.
They will recall your abundant goodness;
age to age shall ring out your justice.

The Lord is kind and full of compassion,
slow to anger, abounding in love.
How good is the Lord to all,
compassionate to all his creatures.

All your creatures shall thank you, O Lord,
and your friends shall repeat their blessing.
They shall speak of the glory of your reign
and declare your might, O God,

to make known to men your mighty deeds
and the glorious splendor of your reign.

THE FATHER'S LOVE IN CHRIST   *John 3:16-17*
God so loved the world that he gave his only Son, in order that whoever believes
in him may not perish but have eternal life. For God sent the Son into the world,
not to condemn the world, but that the world might be saved through him.

Yours is an everlasting kingdom;
your rule lasts from age to age.

The Lord is faithful in all his words
and loving in all his deeds.
The Lord supports all who fall
and raises all who are bowed down.

The eyes of all creatures look to you
and you give them their food in due time.
You open wide your hand,
grant the desires of all who live.

The Lord is just in all his ways
and loving in all his deeds.
He is close to all who call him,
who call on him from their hearts.

He grants the desires of those who fear him,
he hears their cry and he saves them.
The Lord protects all who love him;
but the wicked he will utterly destroy.

Let me speak the praise of the Lord,
let all mankind bless his holy name
forever, for ages unending.

Blessed are you, Father of Jesus Christ,
God, full of kindness and compassion,
God, abounding in love for all creatures!
Help us to understand, we beg you,
that your grandeur is the grandeur of your compassion,
your eternity, the eternity of your faithfulness,
your immensity, the immensity of your love,
through Jesus Christ, in your Holy Spirit,
forever and ever.

THE GOD OF THE POOR

My soul, give praise to the Lord;
I will praise the Lord all my days,
make music to my God while I live.

Put no trust in princes,
in mortal men in whom there is no help.
Take their breath, they return to clay
and their plans that day come to nothing.

He is happy who is helped by Jacob's God,
whose hope is in the Lord his God,
who alone made heaven and earth,
the seas and all they contain.

It is he who keeps faith forever,
who is just to those who are oppressed.
It is he who gives bread to the hungry,
the Lord, who sets prisoners free,

the Lord, who gives sight to the blind,
who raises up those who are bowed down,
the Lord, who protects the stranger
and upholds the widow and orphan.

It is the Lord who loves the just
but thwarts the path of the wicked.
The Lord will reign forever,
Zion's God, from age to age.

Blessed are you, God our Father,
through your Son Jesus Christ,
in the love of the Holy Spirit!
Give us, every day of our lives,
souls filled with thanks to you
and hearts rejoicing in your praise.
We are prisoners of our sins: set us free.
We are oppressed by sadness: give us your joy.
We are strangers and transients in this world:
make us fellow citizens with the saints in heaven,
where you reign, God of Zion, from age to age.

TO THE MARVELOUS GOD

Praise the Lord for he is good;
sing to our God for he is loving:
to him our praise is due.

The Lord builds up Jerusalem
and brings back Israel's exiles,
he heals the brokenhearted,
he binds up all their wounds.
He fixes the number of the stars;
he calls each one by its name.

Our Lord is great and almighty;
his wisdom can never be measured.
The Lord raises the lowly;
he humbles the wicked to the dust.
O sing to the Lord, giving thanks;
sing psalms to our God with the harp.

He covers the heavens with clouds;
he prepares the rain for the earth,
making mountains sprout with grass
and with plants to serve man's needs.

He provides the beasts with their food
and young ravens that call upon him.

His delight is not in horses
nor his pleasure in warriors' strength.
The Lord delights in those who revere him,
in those who wait for his love.

God, our God, you indeed are a marvelous God!
You call each star by its name;
you feed the young ravens;
you heal the brokenhearted;
you rebuild Jerusalem.
Help us proclaim through all our lives
how marvelous you are as God, our God,
in Jesus Christ, with the Holy Spirit, forever and ever.

THE RAVENS OF THE GOOD LORD　　　　　　　　　　　　*Luke 12:22-24*
Jesus said to his disciples, "I tell you, do not be anxious about your life, what you
shall eat, nor about your body, what you shall put on. Life is more than food, and
the body more than clothing. Consider the ravens; they do not sow nor reap; they
have neither cellar nor barn; and yet God feeds them!"

PRAISE THE LORD, JERUSALEM

O praise the Lord, Jerusalem!
Zion, praise your God!

He has strengthened the bars of your gates,
he has blessed the children within you.
He established peace on your borders,
he feeds you with finest wheat.

He sends out his word to the earth
and swiftly runs his command.
He showers down snow white as wool,
he scatters hoarfrost like ashes.

He hurls down hailstones like crumbs.
The waters are frozen at his touch;
he sends forth his word and it melts them:
at the breath of his mouth the waters flow.

He makes his word known to Jacob,
to Israel his laws and decrees.
He has not dealt thus with other nations;
he has not taught them his decrees.

Blessed are you, Lord our God,
builder of the Jerusalem of heaven!

Multiply the children of your Church,
fill them with the best of wheat,
send them your Word, Jesus Christ.

Let your heavenly peace
descend on the earthly Jerusalem;
so that, on the day you have decreed,
everyone will render praise in it
to the God of Jacob and the Father of Jesus Christ.

THE NEW JERUSALEM   *Revelation 21:9...22*
An angel spoke to me, "Come, I will show you the Bride, the Wife of the Lamb."...
He showed me the holy city Jerusalem, coming down out of heaven from God. It
gleamed with the splendor of God.... The wall was built of jasper. The city was of
pure gold, crystal clear.... The twelve gates were twelve pearls, each of the gates
made of a single pearl. The streets of the city were pure gold, transparent as
crystal. I saw no temple in the city. Its temple is the Lord God, the Almighty, and
the Lamb.

SONG OF THE UNIVERSE

Praise the Lord from the heavens,
praise him in the heights.
Praise him, all his angels,
praise him, all his host.

Praise him, sun and moon,
praise him, shining stars.
Praise him, highest heavens
and the waters above the heavens.

Let them praise the name of the Lord.
He commanded: they were made.
He fixed them forever,
gave a law which shall not pass away.

Praise the Lord from the earth,
sea creatures and all oceans,
fire and hail, snow and mist,
stormy winds that obey his word;

all mountains and hills,
all fruit trees and cedars,
beasts, wild and tame,
reptiles and birds on the wing;

all earth's kings and peoples,
earth's princes and rulers;
young men and maidens,
old men together with children.

Let them praise the name of the Lord
for he alone is exalted.
The splendor of his name
reaches beyond heaven and earth.

He exalts the strength of his people.
He is the praise of all his saints,
of the sons of Israel,
of the people to whom he comes close.

With all the creatures of your universe,
may each moment of our lives
sing the glory of your love
in Jesus Christ, the firstborn of all creation!

JESUS CHRIST, THE FIRSTBORN OF THE CREATION   *Colossians 1:15-16*
He — Jesus Christ — is the image of the invisible God, the firstborn of all
creation. For in him were created all things in heaven and on earth, visible and
invisible.

SING A NEW SONG

Sing a new song to the Lord,
his praise in the assembly of the faithful.
Let Israel rejoice in its Maker,
let Zion's sons exult in their king.
Let them praise his name with dancing
and make music with timbrel and harp.

For the Lord takes delight in his people.
He crowns the poor with salvation.

Let the faithful rejoice in their glory,
shout for joy and take their rest.
Let the praise of God be on their lips,...
this honor is for all his faithful.

Lord Jesus,
you wish that your joy be in us,
and that this joy may be complete.
We pray to you:
Stir up the enthusiasm of the Holy Spirit
in the heart of your Church!
May she avoid useless lamentations
that disfigure the beauty of your face!
May she be the homeland of happiness for all peoples!
May she praise you with dance and drum,
may she celebrate with timbrels and harps!
By being at the service of all,
for the sake of the Gospel,
may she repeat for you each day
the new song of her love.

SING A NEW SONG   *Saint Augustine*
O children of peace, children of the Church, one and catholic, walk in the way
that is Christ! Sing on the way as pilgrims do to console themselves in the fatigue
of the journey. Sing on the way! I implore you, through him who is our way, sing a
new song! Do not sing those old songs, harping on the same tune. Instead sing
the love songs of your homeland! Do not sing even one old tune! Since you are a
new person walking on a new path, sing a new song!

Enarratio in Psalm LXVI:6. Corpus Christianorum, Series Latina,
XXXIX, p. 863.

FINAL DOXOLOGY

Alleluia!

Praise God in his holy place,
praise him in his mighty heavens.
Praise him for his powerful deeds,
praise his surpassing greatness.

O praise him with sound of trumpet,
praise him with lute and harp.
Praise him with timbrel and dance,
praise him with strings and pipes.

O praise him with resounding cymbals,
praise him with clashing of cymbals.
Let everything that lives and that breathes
give praise to the Lord. Alleluia!

Blessed are you, Father of Jesus and Source of the Spirit!

All beauty is a spark of the fire of your splendor,
all music is an echo of your harmony,
all kindness is a fragment of your excellence,
all creatures praise your love!

May you be blessed, Father,
by the dew of the morning and the damp fragrance of the evening,
by the song of the nightingale and the perfume of the rose,
by the smile of our children and the grace of our girls,
by the daring of youth and the wisdom of elders,
by the love of the husband and the tenderness of the wife,
by the peace of the pardoned sinner,
and by the holiness of the people in the street!

Blessed are you, especially blessed,
by the humble and poor heart
that trembles with love for you!

May every creature that has breath sing your praise.
May every instant of our life shout "Alleluia" to your glory!

Through Christ, in him, with him,
in the unity of the Holy Spirit,
all glory and honor is yours, Almighty Father,
forever and ever!

ONE GOD AND ONE LORD   *1 Corinthians 8:6*
There is one God, the Father, from whom all things come and for whom we exist.
There is one Lord, Jesus Christ, through whom all things are and through whom
we exist.

1 CHRONICLES 29:10-13
BLESSED MAY YOU BE, O LORD

Prayer of David

Blessed may you be, O LORD,
God of Israel our father,
from eternity to eternity.

Yours, O LORD, are grandeur and power,
majesty, splendor, and glory.
For all in heaven and on earth is yours;
yours, O LORD, is the sovereignty;
you are exalted as head over all.

Riches and honor are from you,
and you have dominion over all.
In your hand are power and might;
it is yours to give grandeur and strength to all.

Therefore, our God, we give you thanks
and we praise the majesty of your name.

SIRACH 36:1, 5, 10-13
COME TO OUR AID, O GOD

Prayer of Sirach

Come to our aid, O God of the universe.
Give new signs and work new wonders;
show forth the splendor of your right hand and arm.

Gather all the tribes of Jacob,
that they may inherit the land as of old.

Show mercy to the people called by your name;
Israel, whom you named your firstborn.

Take pity on your holy city,
Jerusalem, your dwelling place.

Fill Zion with your majesty,
your temple with your glory.

DANIEL 3:26-27, 29-30, 34-41

WITH CONTRITE HEART AND HUMBLE SPIRIT

Prayer of Azariah

Blessed are you, and praiseworthy,
O Lord, the God of our fathers,
and glorious forever is your name.

For you are just in all you have done;
all your deeds are faultless, all your ways right,
and all your judgments proper.

For we have sinned and transgressed
by departing from you,
and we have done every kind of evil.

Your commandments we have not heeded or observed,
nor have we done as you ordered us for our good.

For your name's sake, do not deliver us up forever,
or make void your covenant.

Do not take away your mercy from us,
for the sake of Abraham, your beloved,
Isaac your servant, and Israel your holy one,

To whom you promised to multiply their offspring
like the stars of heaven,
or the sand on the shore of the sea.

For we are reduced, O Lord, beyond any other nation,
brought low everywhere in the world this day
because of our sins.

We have in our day no prince, prophet, or leader,
no holocaust, sacrifice, oblation, or incense,
no place to offer first fruits, to find favor with you.

But with contrite heart and humble spirit
let us be received;

As though it were holocausts of rams and bullocks,
or thousands of fat lambs,

So let our sacrifice be in your presence today
as we follow you unreservedly;
for those who trust in you cannot be put to shame.

And now we follow you with our whole heart,
we fear you and we pray to you.

DANIEL 3:57...88, 56

SONG OF ALL CREATION

Bless the Lord, all you works of the Lord.
Angels of the Lord, bless the Lord.
You heavens, bless the Lord;
praise and exalt him above all forever.

All you waters above the heavens, bless the Lord.
All you hosts of the Lord, bless the Lord.
Sun and moon, bless the Lord;
praise and exalt him above all forever.

Stars of heaven, bless the Lord.
Every shower and dew, bless the Lord.
All you winds, bless the Lord;
praise and exalt him above all forever.

Fire and heat, bless the Lord.
Cold and chill, bless the Lord.
Dew and rain, bless the Lord;
praise and exalt him above all forever.

Frost and chill, bless the Lord.
Ice and snow, bless the Lord.
Nights and days, bless the Lord;
praise and exalt him above all forever.

Light and darkness, bless the Lord.
Lightnings and clouds, bless the Lord.
Let the earth bless the Lord,
praise and exalt him above all forever.

Mountains and hills, bless the Lord.
Everything growing from the earth, bless the Lord.
You springs, bless the Lord;
praise and exalt him above all forever.

Seas and rivers, bless the Lord.
You dolphins and all water creatures, bless the Lord.
All you birds of the air, bless the Lord;
praise and exalt him above all forever.

All you beasts, wild and tame, bless the Lord.
You sons of men, bless the Lord;
praise and exalt him above all forever.

O Israel, bless the Lord.
Priests of the Lord, bless the Lord.
Servants of the Lord, bless the Lord;
praise and exalt him above all forever.

Spirits and souls of the just, bless the Lord.
Holy men of humble heart, bless the Lord.
Hananiah, Azariah, Mishael, bless the Lord;
praise and exalt him above all forever.

Blessed are you in the firmament of heaven,
praiseworthy and glorious forever.

DANIEL 3:52...59, 90

THE THREE YOUTHS' SONG OF PRAISE

Blessed are you, O Lord, the God of our fathers.
And blessed is your holy and glorious name,
praiseworthy and exalted above all for all ages.

Blessed are you in the temple of your holy glory.
Blessed are you who look into the depths
from your throne upon the cherubim,
praiseworthy and exalted above all forever.

Blessed are you in the firmament of heaven.
Bless the Lord, all you works of the Lord;
praise and exalt him above all forever.

Angels of the Lord, bless the Lord.
You heavens, bless the Lord;
praise and exalt him above all forever.

Bless the God of gods, all you who fear the Lord;
praise him and give him thanks,
because his mercy endures forever.

ISAIAH 12:1-6

CANTICLE OF ISAIAH

I give you thanks, O LORD;
though you have been angry with me,
your anger has abated, and you have consoled me.

God indeed is my savior; I am confident and unafraid.
My strength and my courage is the LORD,
and he has been my savior.

With joy you will draw water
at the fountain of salvation,
and say on that day:

Give thanks to the LORD, acclaim his name;
among the nations make known his deeds,
proclaim how exalted is his name.

Sing praise to the LORD for his glorious achievement;
let this be known throughout all the earth.
Shout with exultation, O city of Zion,
for great in your midst is the Holy One of Israel!

JUDITH 16:13-16

CANTICLE OF JUDITH

A new hymn I will sing to my God.
O LORD, great are you and glorious,
wonderful in power and unsurpassable.

Let your every creature serve you;
for you spoke, and they were made.
You sent forth your spirit, and they were created;
no one can resist your word.

The mountains to their bases, and the seas, are shaken;
the rocks, like wax, melt before your glance.
But to those who fear you, you are very merciful.

Though the sweet odor of every sacrifice is a trifle,
and the fat of all holocausts but little in your sight,
one who fears the LORD is forever great.

MATTHEW 5:3-12

THE BEATITUDES

Blest are those who are invited
to the banquet of the Kingdom!

How blest are the poor in spirit:
the reign of God is theirs.

Blest too are the sorrowing;
they shall be consoled.

Blest are the lowly;
they shall inherit the land.

Blest are they who hunger and thirst for holiness;
they shall have their fill.

Blest are they who show mercy;
mercy shall be theirs.

Blest are the single-hearted
for they shall see God.

Blest too the peacemakers;
they shall be called sons of God.

Blest are those persecuted for holiness' sake;
the reign of God is theirs.

Blest are you when they insult you and persecute you
and utter every kind of slander against you because of me.

Be glad and rejoice,
for your reward is great in heaven.

Blest are those who are invited
to the banquet of the Kingdom!

PHILIPPIANS 2:6-11

SONG OF THE PASCHAL MYSTERY

Though he was in the form of God,
he did not deem equality with God
something to be grasped at.

Rather, he emptied himself,
and took the form of a slave,
being born in the likeness of men.

He was known to be of human estate,
and it was thus that he humbled himself,
obediently accepting even death, death on a cross!

Because of this, God highly exalted him
and bestowed on him the name above every other name,

So that at Jesus' name every knee must bend,
in the heavens, on the earth, and under the earth,
and every tongue proclaim
to the glory of God the Father:
JESUS CHRIST IS LORD!

REVELATION 4:11; 5:9-10, 12

SONG TO THE CREATOR AND THE REDEEMER

O Lord our God, you are worthy
to receive glory and honor and power!

For you have created all things;
by your will they came to be and were made!

Worthy are you to receive the scroll
and break open its seals,
for you were slain.

With your blood you purchased for God
men of every race and tongue,
of every people and nation.

You made of them a kingdom,
and priests to serve our God,
and they shall reign on the earth.

Worthy is the Lamb that was slain
to receive power and riches, wisdom and strength,
honor and glory and praise!

The Canticles of Mary, Simeon, and Zechariah may be found on pages 112-113.

PART THREE
CELEBRATION
OF THE
WORD OF GOD

NOTE

CELEBRATION OF THE WORD OF GOD

The celebration of the Word of God, according to liturgical tradition, normally includes
—the proclamation of this Word,
—the homily (eventually in dialogue form), which applies the Word for the benefit of the celebrating community,
—the silent meditation, during which each person conforms his heart to the Word and prays, "Speak, Lord, your servant hears" (1 Sm 3:10).

CHOICE OF TEXTS

To celebrate the Word, you may read
—a text taken from the readings of the liturgy of the day, *or*
—a text chosen at your discretion from the treasury of the Scriptures for the needs of the community, *or*
—a text chosen from those presented on pages 95-111. The selection of these texts is limited intentionally to those that are among the most important ones of God's revelation.

IMPORTANCE AND SIGNIFICANCE OF THE CELEBRATION OF THE WORD OF GOD

—In the Christian religion, whose message comes from heaven and whose Messiah is the Son of God, the essential point is not what we think about God, but rather what God thinks and reveals about himself. Just as the hearing of the Word constitutes the Church, so the hearing of the Word is essential to Christian prayer. It is indeed the highest form of prayer. The most prayerful person, according to revelation, is not the one who talks the most to God, but the one who opens his heart and maintains the deepest silence in order to listen to God.

—In the Christian religion, whose message takes the flesh of human words and whose Messiah is also human, the essence of prayer cannot be reduced to a passive hearing of this Word that has descended from heaven. The essence is rather the welcoming and the planting of the Word in the soil of our hearts, its incarnation in our day-to-day life, its actualization through obedience.

—That is how the religion that is most divine, most heavenly, and most spiritual is also the most human, the most earthly, and the most fully incarnated in our flesh.

OLD TESTAMENT

IN THE IMAGE OF GOD   *Genesis 1:27, 31*
God created man in his image;
in the divine image he created him;
male and female he created them....
God looked at everything he had made,
and he found it very good.

A KINGDOM OF PRIESTS   *Exodus 19:5-6*
Thus says the Lord, "If you hearken to my voice and keep my covenant,
you shall be my special possession, dearer to me than all other people,
though all the earth is mine. You shall be to me a kingdom of priests, a
holy nation."

THE COVENANT   *Exodus 24:7-8*
Moses took the book of the covenant and read it aloud to the people, who
answered, "All that the LORD has said, we will heed and do." Then he
took the blood and sprinkled it on the people saying, "This is the blood
of the covenant which the LORD has made with you in accordance with
all these words of his."

A MERCIFUL GOD   *Exodus 34:5-7*
Having come down in a cloud, the LORD stood with him [Moses] there
and proclaimed his name, "LORD." Thus the LORD passed before him
and cried out, "The LORD, the LORD, a merciful and gracious God, slow
to anger and rich in kindness and fidelity, continuing his kindness for a
thousand generations, and forgiving wickedness and crime and sin."

BE HOLY   *Leviticus 19:1-2*
The LORD said to Moses, "Speak to the whole Israelite community and
tell them: Be holy, for I, the LORD, your God, am holy."

YOU SHALL LOVE THE ALIEN   *Leviticus 19:33-34*

Thus speaks the Lord, "When an alien resides with you in your land, do not molest him. You shall treat the alien who resides with you no differently than the natives born among you; have the same love for him as for yourself; for you too were once aliens in the land of Egypt. I, the LORD, am your God."

YOU SHALL LOVE THE LORD YOUR GOD   *Deuteronomy 6:4-6*

Hear, O Israel! The LORD is our God, the LORD alone! Therefore, you shall love the LORD, your God, with all your heart, and with all your soul, and with all your strength. Take to heart these words which I enjoin on you today.

BECAUSE THE LORD LOVED YOU   *Deuteronomy 7:7-8*

It was not because you are the largest of all nations that the LORD set his heart on you and chose you, for you are really the smallest of all nations. It was because the LORD loved you and because of his fidelity to the oath he had sworn to your fathers, that he brought you out with his strong hand from the place of slavery, and ransomed you from the hand of Pharaoh, king of Egypt.

THE TEST   *Deuteronomy 13:4-5*

The LORD, your God, is testing you to learn whether you really love him with all your heart and with all your soul. The LORD, your God, shall you follow, and him shall you fear; his commandment shall you observe, and his voice shall you heed, serving him and holding fast to him alone.

SPEAK, LORD!   *1 Samuel 3:10*

The LORD came and revealed his presence to Samuel, calling out, "Samuel, Samuel!" Samuel answered, "Speak, for your servant is listening."

THE BETTER SACRIFICE   *1 Samuel 15:22*

Does the LORD so delight in holocausts and sacrifices
as in obedience to the command of the LORD?
Obedience is better than sacrifice,
and submission than the fat of rams.

IN THE NAME OF THE LORD   *1 Samuel 17:45, 47*
David spoke to Goliath, the Philistine, "You come against me with
sword and spear and scimitar, but I come against you in the name of the
LORD of hosts, the God of the armies of Israel that you have insulted....
All this multitude, too, shall learn that it is not by sword or spear that
the LORD saves. For the battle is the LORD'S, and he shall deliver you
into our hands."

IN THE HANDS OF THE LORD   *2 Samuel 24:14*
David spoke to the prophet Gad, "I am in very serious difficulty. Let us
fall by the hand of God, for he is most merciful."

YOUR GOD WILL BE MY GOD   *Ruth 1:16, 22*
Ruth spoke to Naomi, "Do not ask me to abandon or forsake you! for
wherever you go I will go, wherever you lodge I will lodge, your people
shall be my people, and your God my God...." Thus it was that Naomi
returned with the Moabite daughter-in-law, Ruth, who accompanied
her back from the plateau of Moab. They arrived in Bethlehem at the
beginning of the barley harvest.

WE GIVE YOU WHAT WE HAVE RECEIVED FROM YOU
                                   1 Chronicles 29:10, 14-15
David blessed the LORD in the presence of the whole assembly, praying
in these words:
   "Blessed may you be, O LORD,
   God of Israel our father,
   from eternity to eternity...."
"But who am I, and who are my people, that we should have the means
to contribute so freely? For everything is from you, and we only give you
what we have received from you. For we stand before you as aliens: we
are only your guests, like all our fathers."

REJOICING IN THE LORD   *Nehemiah 8:10*
Ezra said to the people, "Today is holy to our LORD. Do not be saddened
this day, for rejoicing in the LORD must be your strength!"

PRAYER OF NEHEMIAH   *Nehemiah 13:22, 31*

Remember in my favor, O my God, and have mercy on me in accordance
with your great mercy!... Remember in my favor, O my God!

BLESSED BE THE NAME OF THE LORD   *Job 1:20-21*

Job cast himself prostrate upon the ground, and said,
"Naked I came forth from my mother's womb,
and naked shall I go back again.
The LORD gave and the LORD has taken away;
blessed be the name of the LORD!"

HAPPY IS THE MAN WHOM GOD REPROVES!   *Job 5:17-18*

Happy is the man whom God reproves!
The Almighty's chastening do not reject.
For he wounds, but he binds up;
he smites, but his hands give healing.

THE CALL OF WISDOM   *Proverbs 1:20, 23, 33*

Wisdom cries aloud in the street,
in the open squares she raises her voice,...
"How long will you turn away at my reproof?...
He who obeys me dwells in security,
in peace, without fear of harm."

FATHER AND MOTHER   *Proverbs 23:22, 24-25*

Listen to your father who begot you,
and despise not your mother when she is old....
The father of a just man will exult with glee;
he who begets a wise son will have joy in him.
Let your father and mother have joy;
let her who bore you exult.

EAT YOUR BREAD WITH JOY   *Ecclesiastes 9:7, 9*

Go, eat your bread with joy and drink your wine with a merry heart,
because it is now that God favors your works.... Enjoy life with the wife
whom you love, all the days of the fleeting life that is granted you under
the sun.

VANITY OF VANITIES   *Ecclesiastes 12:5, 7-8*
Man goes to his lasting home,...
and the dust returns to the earth as it once was,
and the life breath returns to God who gave it.
Vanity of vanities, says Qoheleth, all things are vanity!

STERN AS DEATH IS LOVE   *Song of Songs 8:6-7*
Set me as a seal on your heart,
as a seal on your arm;
For stern as death is love,...
its flames are a blazing fire.
Deep waters cannot quench love,
nor floods sweep it away.

GOD DID NOT MAKE DEATH   *Wisdom 1:13-14*
God did not make death,
nor does he rejoice in the destruction of the living.
For he fashioned all things that they might have being;
and the creatures of the world are wholesome,
and there is not a destructive drug among them.

YOU PERMIT REPENTANCE   *Wisdom 12:19, 22*
You gave your sons good ground for hope
that you would permit repentance for their sins....
You chastise us...
that we may think earnestly of your goodness when we judge,
and, when being judged, may look for mercy.

BREAD FROM HEAVEN   *Wisdom 16:20-21*
You nourished your people with food of angels
and furnished them bread from heaven,
ready to hand, untoiled-for,
endowed with all delights and conforming to every taste.
For this substance of yours revealed
your sweetness toward your children.

INTO THE HANDS OF THE LORD   *Sirach 2:17-18*

Those who fear the LORD prepare their hearts
and humble themselves before him.
Let us fall into the hands of the LORD
and not into the hands of men,
For equal to his majesty
is the mercy that he shows.

THE COMING OF THE KING OF JUSTICE   *Isaiah 11:1-2, 5*

A shoot shall sprout from the stump of Jesse,
and from his roots a bud shall blossom.
The spirit of the LORD shall rest upon him:
a spirit of wisdom and of understanding,
A spirit of counsel and of strength,
a spirit of knowledge and of fear of the LORD....
Justice shall be the band around his waist,
and faithfulness a belt upon his hips.

THE MESSIANIC FEAST   *Isaiah 25:6-8*

On this mountain the LORD of hosts
will provide for all peoples
A feast of rich food and choice wines,
juicy, rich food and pure, choice wines.
On this mountain he will destroy
the veil that veils all peoples,
The web that is woven over all nations;
he will destroy death forever.
The Lord GOD will wipe away the tears from all faces.

CAN A MOTHER FORGET HER INFANT?   *Isaiah 49:14-16*

Zion said, "The LORD has forsaken me;
my LORD has forgotten me."
Can a mother forget her infant,
be without tenderness for the child of her womb?
Even should she forget,
I will never forget you.
See, upon the palms of my hands I have written your name.

WITH ENDURING LOVE   *Isaiah 54:8, 10*

With enduring love I take pity on you,
says the LORD, your redeemer....
Though the mountains leave their place
and the hills be shaken,
My love shall never leave you
nor my covenant of peace be shaken,
says the LORD, who has mercy on you.

THE ONE WHOM I APPROVE   *Isaiah 66:1-2*

The heavens are my throne,
the earth is my footstool....
My hand made all these things
when all of them came to be, says the LORD.
This is the one whom I approve:
the lowly and afflicted man who trembles at my word.

CALLING   *Jeremiah 1:4-5, 8*

The word of the LORD came to me thus:
Before I formed you in the womb I knew you,
before you were born I dedicated you....
Have no fear before them,
because I am with you to deliver you, says the LORD.

BLESSED IS THE MAN   *Jeremiah 17:5-8*

Thus says the LORD:
Cursed is the man who trusts in human beings,
who seeks his strength in flesh,
whose heart turns away from the LORD.
He is like a barren bush in the desert....
Blessed is the man who trusts in the LORD,
whose hope is the LORD.
He is like a tree planted beside the waters
that stretches out its roots to the stream.

THE NEW COVENANT   *Jeremiah 31:31, 33*

The days are coming, says the LORD, when I will make a new covenant
with the house of Israel.... I will place my law within them, and write it
upon their hearts; I will be their God, and they shall be my people.

HOPE IN SILENCE   *Lamentations 3:22-26*
The favors of the LORD are not exhausted,
his mercies are not spent;
They are renewed each morning,
so great is his faithfulness.
My portion is the LORD, says my soul;
therefore will I hope in him.
Good is the LORD to one who waits for him,
to the soul that seeks him;
It is good to hope in silence
for the saving help of the LORD.

A NEW HEART   *Ezekiel 36:25-27*
Thus says the Lord, "I will sprinkle clean water upon you to cleanse you
from all your impurities, and from all your idols I will cleanse you. I
will give you a new heart and place a new spirit within you, taking from
your bodies your stony hearts and giving you natural hearts. I will put
my spirit within you."

I WILL OPEN YOUR GRAVES   *Ezekiel 37:12-14*
Thus says the Lord GOD: O my people, I will open your graves and have
you rise from them, and bring you back to the land of Israel. Then you
shall know that I am the LORD, when I open your graves and have you
rise from them, O my people! I will put my spirit in you that you may
live.

GOD OF WISDOM   *Daniel 2:19-22*
Daniel blessed the God of heaven and said,
"Blessed be the name of God forever and ever,
for wisdom and power are his.
He causes the changes of the times and seasons,
makes kings and unmakes them.
He gives wisdom to the wise
and knowledge to those who understand.
He reveals deep and hidden things
and knows what is in the darkness,
for the light dwells with him."

I WILL ESPOUSE YOU TO ME FOREVER   *Hosea 2:21-22*

Thus says the Lord,
"I will espouse you to me forever:
I will espouse you in right and in justice,
in love and in mercy;
I will espouse you in fidelity,
and you shall know the LORD."

WHEN ISRAEL WAS A CHILD   *Hosea 11:1, 3-4*

Thus says the Lord,
"When Israel was a child I loved him,
out of Egypt I called my son....
Yet it was I who taught Ephraim to walk,
who took them in my arms;
I drew them with human cords,
with bands of love;
I fostered them like one
who raises an infant to his cheeks;
Yet, though I stooped to feed my child,
they did not know that I was their healer."

I WILL POUR OUT MY SPIRIT   *Joel 3:1-2*

Thus says the Lord,
"I will pour out my spirit upon all mankind.
Your sons and daughters shall prophesy,
your old men shall dream dreams,
your young men shall see visions;
Even upon the servants and the handmaids,
in those days, I will pour out my spirit."

MEET YOUR GOD   *Amos 4:12*

Thus says the Lord,
"Prepare to meet your God, O Israel."

HE WHO FORMED THE MOUNTAINS   *Amos 4:13*

He who formed the mountains, and created the wind,
and declares to man his thoughts;

Who made the dawn and the darkness,
and strides upon the heights of the earth:
The LORD, the God of hosts, this is his name.

AWAY WITH YOUR SONGS *Amos 5:23-24*
Thus says the Lord,
"Away with your noisy songs!
I will not listen to the melodies of your harps.
But if you would offer me holocausts,
then let justice surge like water,
and goodness like an unfailing stream."

FAMINE AND THIRST FOR THE WORD OF THE LORD *Amos 8:11*
Yes, days are coming, says the Lord GOD,
when I will send famine upon the land:
Not a famine of bread, or thirst for water,
but for hearing the word of the LORD.

WHAT THE LORD REQUIRES OF YOU *Micah 6:8*
You have been told, O man, what is good,
and what the LORD requires of you:
Only to do the right and to love goodness,
and to walk humbly with your God.

GOD DELIGHTS IN CLEMENCY *Micah 7:18-19*
Who is there like you, the God who removes guilt
and pardons sin for the remnant of his inheritance;
Who does not persist in anger forever,
but delights rather in clemency,
And will again have compassion on us,
treading underfoot our guilt?
You will cast into the depths of the sea all our sins.

THE JUST MAN, BECAUSE OF HIS FAITH, SHALL LIVE
Habakkuk 2:1-2, 4
I will keep watch to see what God will say to me,
and what answer he will give to my complaint.

Then the LORD answered me and said:...
"The rash man has no integrity;
but the just man, because of his faith, shall live."

SEEK THE LORD   *Zephaniah 2:3*
Seek the LORD, all you humble of the earth,
who have observed his law;
Seek justice, seek humility;
perhaps you may be sheltered
on the day of the LORD's anger.

SHOUT FOR JOY, O DAUGHTER OF ZION   *Zephaniah 3:14, 16-17*
Shout for joy, O daughter of Zion!...
Fear not, O Zion, be not discouraged!
The LORD, your God, is in your midst, a mighty savior;
He will rejoice over you with gladness,
and renew you in his love.

THE FAITHFUL CITY   *Zechariah 8:3, 8*
Thus says the LORD:
"I will return to Zion,
and I will dwell within Jerusalem;
Jerusalem shall be called the faithful city,
and the mountain of the LORD of hosts,
the holy mountain....
They shall be my people, and I will be their God,
with faithfulness and justice."

NEW TESTAMENT

THE CHRISTIAN PRAYER   *Matthew 6:7-9*

Jesus said to his disciples, "In your prayer do not rattle on like the pagans. They think they will win a hearing by the sheer multiplication of words. Do not imitate them. Your Father knows what you need before you ask him. This is how you are to pray: 'Our Father in heaven.' "

THE COMMUNITY PRAYER   *Matthew 18:19-20*

Jesus said to his disciples, "Again I tell you, if two of you join your voices on earth to pray for anything whatever, it shall be granted you by my Father in heaven. Where two or three are gathered in my name, there am I in their midst."

THE PRAYER OF MARY, MOTHER OF JESUS   *Luke 1:46-47*

Mary said:

"My being proclaims the greatness of the Lord,
my spirit finds joy in God my savior!"

THE PRAYER OF MARY, SISTER OF MARTHA   *Luke 10:38-39*

On their journey Jesus entered a village where a woman named Martha welcomed him to her home. She had a sister named Mary, who seated herself at the Lord's feet and listened to his words.

THE PRAYER OF THE TAX COLLECTOR   *Luke 18:13-14*

The tax collector kept his distance, not even daring to raise his eyes to heaven. All he did was beat his breast and say, "O God, be merciful to me, a sinner." Believe me, the Lord said, this man went home from the temple justified but the Pharisee did not. For everyone who exalts himself shall be humbled while he who humbles himself shall be exalted.

THE PRAYER OF THE GOOD THIEF *Luke 23:42-43*

He said, "Jesus, remember me when you enter upon your reign." And Jesus replied, "I assure you: this day you will be with me in paradise."

THE PRAYER OF JESUS: HYMN OF PRAISE *Luke 10:21-22*

Jesus rejoiced in the Holy Spirit and said: "I offer you praise, O Father, Lord of heaven and earth, because what you have hidden from the learned and the clever you have revealed to the merest children. Yes, Father, you have graciously willed it so!"

THE PRAYER OF JESUS: THAT THEY MAY BE ONE
John 17:1, 11, 21

Jesus looked up to heaven and said:... "O Father most holy, protect them with your name which you have given me [that they may be one, even as we are one]... that the world may believe that you sent me."

THE PRAYER OF JESUS IN GETHSEMANI *Mark 14:36*

Jesus said, "Abba (O Father), you have the power to do all things. Take this cup away from me. But let it be as you would have it, not as I."

THE PRAYER OF JESUS ON THE CROSS *Mark 15:34; Luke 23:46*

Jesus cried in a loud voice,
"My God, my God, why have you forsaken me?"
"Father, into your hands I commend my spirit."

THE PRAYER OF THE EARLY COMMUNITY *Acts 1:14*

Together they devoted themselves to constant prayer. There were some women in their company, and Mary the mother of Jesus.

THE LOVE OF CHRIST   *Romans 8:35, 37-39*

Who will separate us from the love of Christ? Trial, or distress, or
persecution, or hunger, or nakedness, or danger, or the sword?... Yet in
all this we are more than conquerors because of him who has loved us.
For I am certain that... [nothing] will be able to separate us from the
love of God that comes to us in Christ Jesus, our Lord.

THE MESSAGE OF THE CROSS   *1 Corinthians 1:18, 23-25*

The message of the cross is complete absurdity to those who are headed
for ruin, but to us who are experiencing salvation it is the power of
God.... We preach Christ crucified—a stumbling block to Jews, and an
absurdity to Gentiles; but to those who are called, Jews and Greeks
alike, Christ the power of God and the wisdom of God. For God's folly is
wiser than men, and his weakness more powerful than men.

ONE AND THE SAME SPIRIT   *1 Corinthians 12:4-6*

There are different gifts but the same Spirit; there are different ministries but the same Lord; there are different works but the same God
who accomplishes all of them in everyone.

THE GOD OF PEACE   *2 Corinthians 13:11*

Mend your ways. Encourage one another. Live in harmony and peace,
and the God of love and peace will be with you.

THE SPIRIT OF OUR HEARTS   *Galatians 4:6-7*

The proof that you are sons is the fact that God has sent forth into our
hearts the spirit of his Son which cries out "Abba!" ("Father!") You are
no longer a slave but a son! And the fact that you are a son makes you an
heir, by God's design.

THE FRUITS OF THE SPIRIT   *Galatians 5:22-25*

In contrast, the fruit of the spirit is love, joy, peace, patient endurance,
kindness, generosity, faith, mildness and chastity. Against such there

is no law! Those who belong to Christ Jesus have crucified their flesh with its passions and desires. Since we live by the spirit, let us follow the spirit's lead.

SALVATION BY HIS FAVOR　　　　　*Ephesians 2:8-9*
It is owing to his favor that salvation is yours through faith. This is not your own doing, it is God's gift; neither is it a reward for anything you have accomplished, so let no one pride himself on it.

ALL THAT IS ADMIRABLE　　　　　*Philippians 4:8-9*
Your thoughts should be wholly directed to all that is true, all that deserves respect, all that is honest, pure, admirable, decent, virtuous, or worthy of praise. Live according to what you have learned and accepted, what you have heard me say and seen me do. Then will the God of peace be with you.

GIVE THANKS TO THE FATHER　　　　　*Colossians 1:12-13*
Give thanks to the Father for having made you worthy to share the lot of the saints in light. He rescued us from the power of darkness and brought us into the kingdom of his beloved Son.

PUT ON LOVE　　　　　*Colossians 3:14-16*
Put on love which binds all virtues together and makes them perfect. Christ's peace must reign in your hearts, since as members of the one body you have been called to that peace. Dedicate yourselves to thankfulness. Let the word of Christ, rich as it is, dwell in you.

REJOICE ALWAYS　　　　　*1 Thessalonians 5:16-18*
Rejoice always, never cease praying, render constant thanks; such is God's will for you in Christ Jesus.

DO NOT STIFLE THE SPIRIT *1 Thessalonians 5:19-21*
Do not stifle the Spirit. Do not despise prophecies. Test everything; retain what is good.

ONE IS THE MEDIATOR *1 Timothy 2:5-6*
The truth is this:
"God is one.
One also is the mediator between God and men,
the man Christ Jesus,
who gave himself as a ransom for all."

REMEMBER JESUS CHRIST *2 Timothy 2:8-9*
Remember that Jesus Christ, a descendant of David, was raised from the dead. This is the gospel I preach; in preaching it I suffer as a criminal, even to the point of being thrown into chains—but there is no chaining the word of God!

GOD'S WORD IS LIVING *Hebrews 4:12*
God's word is living and effective, sharper than any two-edged sword. It penetrates and divides soul and spirit, joints and marrow; it judges the reflections and thoughts of the heart.

GOD CHOSE THE POOR *James 2:5*
Did not God choose those who are poor in the eyes of the world to be rich in faith and heirs of the kingdom he promised to those who love him?

THE MERCIFUL JUDGMENT *James 2:12-13*
Always speak and act as people destined for judgment under the law of freedom. Merciless is the judgment on the one who has not shown mercy; but mercy triumphs over judgment.

THE SPIRIT IN ITS GLORY   *1 Peter 4:13-14*

Rejoice in the measure that you share Christ's sufferings. When his glory is revealed, you will rejoice exultantly. Happy are you when you are insulted for the sake of Christ, for then God's Spirit in its glory has come to rest on you.

THE MORNING STAR   *2 Peter 1:19*

We possess the prophetic message as something altogether reliable. Keep your attention closely fixed on it, as you would on a lamp shining in a dark place until the first streaks of dawn appear and the morning star rises in your hearts.

GOD IS LOVE   *1 John 4:16*

We have come to know and to believe in the love God has for us. God is love, and he who abides in love abides in God, and God in him.

WELCOME THE MERCY OF OUR LORD   *Jude 20-21*

Beloved, grow strong in your holy faith through prayer in the Holy Spirit. Persevere in God's love, and welcome the mercy of our Lord Jesus Christ which leads to life eternal.

I STAND AT THE DOOR   *Revelation 3:19-20*

Whoever is dear to me I reprove and chastise. Be earnest about it, therefore. Repent! Here I stand, knocking at the door. If anyone hears me calling and opens the door, I will enter his house and have supper with him, and he with me.

COME, LORD JESUS!   *Revelation 22:20-21*

The One who gives this testimony says, "Yes, I am coming soon!" Amen! Come, Lord Jesus! The grace of the Lord Jesus be with you all. Amen!

CANTICLE OF MARY

Luke 1:46-55

My soul proclaims the greatness of the Lord,
my spirit rejoices in God my Savior;
for he has looked with favor on his lowly servant.

From this day all generations will call me blessed:
the Almighty has done great things for me,
and holy is his Name.

He has mercy on those who fear him
in every generation.

He has shown the strength of his arm,
he has scattered the proud in their conceit.

He has cast down the mighty from their thrones,
and has lifted up the lowly.

He has filled the hungry with good things,
and the rich he has sent away empty.

He has come to the help of his servant Israel,
for he has remembered his promise of mercy,
the promise he made to our fathers,
to Abraham and his children forever.

CANTICLE OF SIMEON

Luke 2:29-32

Lord, now you let your servant go in peace;
your word has been fulfilled:

My own eyes have seen the salvation
which you have prepared in the sight of every people:

A light to reveal you to the nations
and the glory of your people Israel.

CANTICLE OF ZECHARIAH

Luke 1:68-79

Blessed be the Lord, the God of Israel;
he has come to his people and set them free.

He has raised up for us a mighty savior,
born of the house of his servant David.

Through his holy prophets he promised of old
that he would save us from our enemies,
from the hands of all who hate us.

He promised to show mercy to our fathers
and to remember his holy covenant.

This was the oath he swore to our father Abraham:
to set us free from the hands of our enemies,
free to worship him without fear,
holy and righteous in his sight
all the days of our life.

You, my child, shall be called the prophet of the Most High,
for you will go before the Lord to prepare his way,
to give his people knowledge of salvation
by the forgiveness of their sins.

In the tender compassion of our God
the dawn from on high shall break upon us,
to shine on those who dwell in darkness and the shadow of death,
and to guide our feet into the way of peace.

EVERY CREATURE IN HEAVEN AND ON EARTH,
UNDER THE EARTH AND IN THE SEA,
AND IN THE WHOLE UNIVERSE,
I HEARD THEM PRAISING:
TO HIM WHO REIGNS UPON THE THRONE
AND TO THE LAMB
PRAISE, HONOR, GLORY, AND MIGHT
FOREVER AND EVER!

Revelation 5:13

PART FOUR

PRAYERS

ADVENT

LET THE DAY COME, LORD

Come, Lord Jesus, come!

Let the day come, Lord,
    when our misery
will find your mercy.

Let the day come, Lord,
    when our poverty
will find your riches.

Let the day come, Lord,
    when our path
will find the way to your house.

Let the day come, Lord,
    when our tears
will find your smile.

Let the day come, Lord,
    when our joy
will find your heaven.

Let the day come, Lord,
    when your Church
will find the Kingdom.

May you be blest, Father,
    for that day
when our eyes will find your face!
    Throughout all the time of our life
you have not ceased to come before us
    in your Son Jesus Christ,
our Savior and our brother.

Let the Day Come, Lord, *Revelation 21:1-4; 22:20.*
O Wisdom (p. 119), *Sirach 24:1-22   Isaiah 9:1   Ezekiel 34:23*
Matthew 1:23   John 10   Ephesians 2:14,20   Revelation 3:7.

O WISDOM

Come, O Lord, come, save your people!

O Wisdom,
issuing from the mouth of the Most High,
announced by the prophets:
Come to teach us the way of salvation,
    Come, O Lord, come, save your people!

O Lord,
shepherd of the house of Israel,
who guide your people:
Come to redeem us by the strength of your arm,
    Come, O Lord, come, save your people!

O Son of David,
standard of people and of kings,
you whom the world implores:
Come to deliver us, Lord, do not delay,
    Come, O Lord, come, save your people!

O Key of David,
and scepter of the house of Israel,
you who open so no one can close,
you who close so no one can open:
Come to free those who wait in the darkness,
    Come, O Lord, come, save your people!

O Rising Sun,
splendor of eternal light and sun of justice:
Come to give light
to those who are seated in the shadow of death,
    Come, O Lord, come, save your people!

O King of nations,
expectation of peoples and cornerstone of the Church:
Come to deliver
those whom you have created,
    Come, O Lord, come, save your people!

O Emmanuel,
King and hope of nations
and Savior of all people:
Come to free us, Lord, do not delay,
    Come, O Lord, come, save your people!

THOSE TRUSTING IN YOU, O LORD

Those trusting in you, O Lord,
will never be deceived.

For the husband or the wife
who awaits the return of one who has left
and will never return,
    we pray to you, Lord.
Those trusting in you, O Lord, will never be deceived.

For parents
awaiting the return of a child
who will never return,
    we pray to you, Lord.
Those trusting in you, O Lord, will never be deceived.

For those who are in prison
awaiting their return home
though they will never return,
    we pray to you, Lord.
Those trusting in you, O Lord, will never be deceived.

For those who are sick
and await the return of their health,
which will never return,
    we pray to you, Lord.
Those trusting in you, O Lord, will never be deceived.

For those who are yearning to die
yet see no end to their suffering,
    we pray to you, Lord.
Those trusting in you, O Lord, will never be deceived.

For the people of Israel
who are still awaiting the Savior
because, in Jesus, they see not his presence,
    we pray to you, Lord.
Those trusting in you, O Lord, will never be deceived.

For those who no longer are waiting for anything,
who do not even know there is a Savior to hope for,
    we pray to you, Lord.
Those trusting in you, O Lord, will never be deceived.

Psalm 25: 3,6.

Lord, God of all trust,
remember your kindness,
remember your love.

Do not deceive, Lord,
those whom life has always deceived
and whose hope is now only in you.
Keep them in the joy of your love,
O you God of all wonders,
who alone can grant our desires
beyond even hope.

HOW LONG THE WAY!

Emmanuel, come, save your people.

How long the path which leads to you!
        Lord, come to meet us,
        be our way.

How heavy the burden of our misery!
        Lord, come to meet us,
        be our rest.

How darkly hard the journey to our star!
        Lord, come to meet us,
        be our sunlight.

How lonely do we wander,
stumbling together in the darkness!
        Lord, come to meet us,
        be our brother.

How long, Lord Jesus, do we wait for your return!
Yet, since you lit hope's flame within our hearts,
come now at last to be our hope's fulfillment.
Allow us to dwell near your heart:
        there we belong
        forever and ever.

IT WILL BE DAYLIGHT SOON

The night passes on,
it will be morning soon.

The hour has come, Lord:
wake us from our sleep.

Allow us to walk with children of light
toward your coming Dawn.

THAT WE MAY BE READY

God, our Father, we pray to you:

Let your grace keep us awake
that our hearts be not dulled
by the cares of life.

Grant us also to pray always
that we may be standing ready
when the Son of Man comes.

LIKE DIRTY LAUNDRY

See, Lord —
our acts of goodness are before you
like dirty laundry,
and we fall like dead leaves
that the wind sweeps away.

But you are our Father —
how could you forget us?
Open the heavens and come down!
Come to save us
through your Son Jesus.

It Will Be Daylight Soon, *Romans 13:11-14,* First Sunday, A.
That We May Be Ready, *Luke 21:34-36,* First Sunday, C.
Like Dirty Laundry, *Isaiah 63:19; 64:5-7,* First Sunday, B.

STAY AWAKE AND PRAY

Lord Jesus, you tell us
to stay awake and pray
because we know
    neither the day nor the hour.

Make each day find us more ready
to welcome you into our lives,
and may the last of our days
    be the happiest,
because we will then return home
and discover the place
that you have prepared for us.

YOUR KINGDOM COME

God our Father:

Your Kingdom come
on earth as in heaven!

May the day come when the morning star
will rise in our hearts!

May the day come when we will see you face to face:
    you, our Father,
with Jesus, our Lord and our brother,
and the Spirit, which dwells in our hearts!

Stay Awake and Pray, *Matthew 24:42,* First Sunday, A.
Your Kingdom Come, *2 Peter 1:19 1 John 3:2.*

YOUR RETURN IS NEAR

"Yes, your return is near!
Oh yes, come, Lord Jesus!"

Soon I am going to see you, O my God,
and I rejoice for that day.

Not for what I am,
not for what I have,
but just because I am nothing
and my hands are empty before you.

Because I depend on you, Lord,
and I rejoice for that great feastday
when my misery will meet
your mercy.

LOVE AND TRUTH EMBRACE

In you, Lord, Jesus, tiny Babe of Bethlehem,
love and truth now meet,
justice and peace now embrace.
In you, Lord, truth reaches up from earth,
and justice leans down from heaven.
Therefore we pray:

Upon this earth, which now is yours,
may every moment of our lives unfold the mystery
of love and truth,
of justice and peace.

Your Return Is Near, *Revelation 22:20.*
Love and Truth Embrace, *Psalm 85:11-12,* Second Sunday, B.

THE PATH OF YOUR RETURN

Lord Jesus,
may you yourself prepare
in the wilderness of our hearts
the path of your return.

The hills of our pride —
tear them down with your humility.
The valleys of our despair —
fill them with your hope.
The winding roads of our lives —
straighten them with your truth,
and let bloom in our desert
    the daffodils of your joy.

Then will we be able to see your glory
    and adore your presence
in the face of each of our brothers and sisters.

AS THE LABORER

Lord Jesus,
you who wait at the gates,
you who are so near to us,
    we pray to you:

Lock deep in our hearts the treasure of patience
until the day of your coming, Lord.

As the laborer waits patiently
    for the precious fruit of the ground,
let us likewise wait,
    in the peace of hope,
for the time of the eternal harvest.

The Path of Your Return, *Isaiah 40:3-5,* Second Sunday, B.
As the Laborer, *James 5:7-9,* Third Sunday, A.

YOUR PEACE BEYOND ALL UNDERSTANDING

God our Father, we pray to you:
Let your peace which is far beyond all understanding
keep our hearts and our thoughts
in expectation of the return of your Son,
    Jesus Christ, our Lord.

HE WHOM NO ONE CAN AWAIT

God our Father,
you are the one we cannot await,
if you yourself do not light the flame in our hearts.

You are the one we cannot desire,
if you yourself do not dwell already in our hearts.

Therefore we pray:
Each day revive in us more and more
the consciousness of our misery,
and fill us unceasingly with your mercy.

Your Peace beyond All Understanding, *Philippians 4:7*, Third Sunday, C.

BLESSINGS FOR THE ADVENT SEASON

May the God of hope fill us
with all the joy and the peace of our faith,
so that we may abound in hope
    by the power of the Holy Spirit!   —*Amen.*

May God our Father strengthen us until the last day
    so that we will be without blame
    in the Day of our Lord Jesus Christ.   —*Amen.*
He is faithful, he who calls us
to fellowship with his Son Jesus, our Lord.   —*Amen.*
To him be glory forever!   —*Amen.*

Marana tha! Come, Lord Jesus!   —*Amen.*
Your grace be with us all.   —*Amen.*

May God our Father,
who has begun an excellent work in us,
see that it is completed
when the Day of Christ Jesus comes!   —*Amen.*
To him be glory forever!   —*Amen.*

May the Lord help us to grow and abound
    in love for one another.   —*Amen.*
May he confirm our hearts in holiness without blame
    before God our Father,
at the time of his coming with all his saints!   —*Amen.*

May the God of peace himself
make us completely holy.   —*Amen.*
May he keep us blameless in spirt, soul and body,
for the coming of our Lord Jesus Christ.   —*Amen.*
Forever faithful is he who calls us — God our Father! —*Amen.*

Expectant, let us live in joyful hope
for the revelation of the glory
of our God and Savior, Christ Jesus!   —*Amen.*
To him be glory forever!   —*Amen.*

Romans 15:13   1 Corinthians 1:8-9; 16:23-24   Philippians 1:6
1 Thessalonians 3:12-13; 5:23-24   Titus 2:12-14.

May we grow in grace and knowledge
of our Lord and Savior Jesus Christ.   —*Amen.*
To him be glory now and in eternity!   —*Amen.*

Amen! Come, Lord Jesus!   —*Amen.*
May your grace be with us all!   —*Amen.*

Each blessing concludes with the usual formula:

May almighty God bless you,
the Father, and the Son, and the Holy Spirit. Amen.

2 Peter 3:18   Revelation 22:21.

CHRISTMAS

AND

EPIPHANY

YOU WHO WISHED TO BE BORN
IN THE MIDST OF OUR SINS

Litany of the Kyrie

You are holy,
you who wished to be born in the midst of our sins
the better to pardon us,
    we beg you:
    Lord, have mercy.

You are strong,
you who wished to be born weak as a child
in order to give us strength,
    we beg you:
    Christ, have mercy.

You are immortal,
you who took on a body to die
in order to give us immortality,
    we beg you:
    Lord, have mercy.

Holy God, strong God, immortal God,
give the peace of heaven to our earth,
and open the door of your mercy
to the beggars of your love.

TODAY THE ANGELS

Glory to God on high!

Today the angels sing in the heavens —
    sing with them!
Glory to God on high!

Today the shepherds come to Bethlehem —
    come with them!
Glory to God on high!

They find Joseph and Mary and the newborn child —
    search with them!
Glory to God on high!

They marvel and give glory to God
for all that they have seen and heard —
    give glory to God!
Glory to God on high!

They proclaim the word that has been told them
concerning the Savior, Messiah, and Lord —
    proclaim Jesus with them!
Glory to God on high!

The Virgin Mary treasures all these things
and ponders them in her heart —
    pray with her!
Glory to God on high!

MAY THEY GIVE YOU GLORY FOR US, O LORD

Praise to you now and evermore!

May they give you glory for us, O Lord —
the Virgin Mary whose child you were,
and the carpenter Joseph who made you his own.
    Praise to you now and evermore!

May they give you glory for us, O Lord —
the angels who, singing, praised your birth,
and the manger wherein, as a child, you lay.
    Praise to you now and evermore!

May they give you glory for us, O Lord —
the shepherds who came to worship you,
and your mother herself, who marvelled at you.
    Praise to you now and evermore!

May they give you glory for us, O Lord —
the Bethlehem infants who died for you,
and the martyrdom of the hearts of their mothers.
    Praise to you now and evermore!

May they give you glory for us, O Lord —
the Wise Men who journeyed from far in the East,
and their brilliant star aloft in your sky.
    Praise to you now and evermore!

May they give you glory for us, O Lord —
old Simeon holding you clasped in his arms,
and Anna the prophetess,
whose age your coming did bless with joy.
    Praise to you now and evermore!

On this day [at this time] of your holy birth,
O Jesus Lord, we pray to you:
Let all our lives bring glory to you,
and because your birth was here on earth,
give us someday our own birth in heaven
        for one eternal Christmas.

O GOD, THE RULER OF AGES ETERNAL

Praise to you, O Lord!

O God, the ruler of ages eternal,
though without beginning or end,
you chose to be born an infant in time.
    Praise to you, O Lord!

O God, the invisible,
you are he whom nobody has seen or can see,
yet you assume the face of the Son of Mary.
    Praise to you, O Lord!

O God, the all-powerful,
you hold the mountains in the palm of your hand,
yet you let yourself be wrapped in swaddling clothes.
    Praise to you, O Lord!

O God, the eternal glory,
innumerable angels acclaim you endlessly,
yet you chose to be rocked to sleep
by the songs of the daughter of David.
    Praise to you, O Lord!

O God, the universal provider,
you feed every creature,
yet you chose to hunger for the milk of your Mother.
    Praise to you, O Lord!

O God, the infinite,
heaven and earth cannot contain you,
yet you rest in the arms of Mary.
    Praise to you, O Lord!

O God, the perfect joy,
you are the source of the happiness of heaven and earth,
yet you cry like a little child.
    Praise to you, O Lord!

O God, the eternal Word,
you are the light of all created intelligence,
yet you are laid in a manger
and cannot even speak.
    Praise to you, O Lord!

FOR ALL WHO GIVE YOU A FACE

Glory to God on high!

For all who give you a face,
    Lord Jesus,
by spreading your love in the world,
    we praise you.

For all who give you hands,
    Lord Jesus,
by doing their best toward their brothers and sisters,
    we praise you.

For all who give you a mouth,
    Lord Jesus,
by defending the weak and the oppressed,
    we praise you.

For all who give you eyes,
    Lord Jesus,
by seeing every bit of love
in the heart of man and woman,
    we praise you.

For all who give you a heart,
    Lord Jesus,
by preferring the poor to the rich,
the weak to the strong,
    we praise you.

For all who give to your poverty,
    Lord Jesus,
the look of hope for the Kingdom,
    we praise you.

For all who reveal you
simply by what they are,
    Lord Jesus,
because they reflect your beauty in their lives,
    we praise you.

God our Father,
you who are the God of a thousand faces,
yet whom nothing can reveal completely
except the face of the child of Bethlehem,
    we pray to you:

Continue in our lives the mystery of Christmas.
Let your Son become flesh in us
so that we may be for all our brothers and sisters
    the revelation of your love.

CHRIST SHOWN FORTH IN THE FLESH

Glory and praise to you,
Lord Jesus Christ!

Christ, shown forth in the flesh,
    Glory and praise to you!
Christ, made just in the Spirit,
    Glory and praise to you!
Christ, who was seen by the angels,
    Glory and praise to you,
        Lord Jesus Christ!

Christ, proclaimed among the nations,
    Glory and praise to you!
Christ, received in faith through all the world,
    Glory and praise to you!
Christ, exalted in glory,
    Glory and praise to you,
        Lord Jesus Christ!

1 Timothy 3:16.

FOR ALL THE CHILDREN OF THE WORLD

Remember us, O Lord, in your loving care.

For all the children everywhere in the world,
that they may find, like the child Jesus,
the love of a father or a mother to welcome them,
    let us pray.

For children who suffer from the wickedness of others,
who are hurt by their hatred or killed by their wars,
that they may find peace and joy close to God, our Father,
    let us pray.

For children who are born infirm,
with a deformed body or a deficient mind,
that they may find beauty of heart
close to God, the source of all splendor,
    let us pray.

For children who are neither wanted nor loved,
that they may know that God their Father
loves them as no one on earth can love them,
    let us pray.

For children who are orphans,
that they may discover in a family who adopts them
the love of their Father in heaven,
    let us pray.

For all children who are born of a beautiful love
and who are happy during Christmastime,
that they may learn to share their happiness,
    let us pray.

    God our Father,
source of all fatherhood in heaven and on earth,
    we pray to you:

Let your love watch over all the children of the world;
let it help them grow in grace and wisdom.

Keep in us, too, a childlike spirit and humility
that we may one day enter your Kingdom.

We ask this of you in the name of Jesus,
who was born for us, a little child in Bethlehem,
and who rules with you forever.

ON THIS DAY OF YOUR BIRTH

On this day [at this time] of your birth, Lord Jesus,
wonderful and adorable child,
we want to praise you and thank you.

You are the unapproachable God,
yet the shepherds meet you in the stable.
No tongue can pronounce your name,
yet Mary calls you "My little one."
You are raised above the heavens,
yet you rest in a manger.
You are the light of all lights,
yet you are born in the nighttime of humankind.

With the angels and shepherds
we surround your manger and sing:
"Glory to God in the highest,
and peace to those whom you love!"

And because you chose to make yours the sorrows
    of our humanity,
give us a share also in the riches of your divinity,
O you, the firstborn of the Virgin Mary,
    and our brother.

ONLY SON, FULL OF GRACE AND TRUTH

(Prologue of John)

Lord Jesus, only Son,
full of grace and truth,
    we pray to you:

You are the Word of your Father —
    reveal him to us!

You are the light that shines in the darkness —
    enlighten us!

You have come into the midst of your own —
    dwell among us!

You give us the power of becoming children of God —
    receive us as brothers and sisters!

You set up your tent among us —
    stay with us!

You are the Son, full of grace and truth —
    save us!

Eternal and almighty God,
King of kings and Lord of lords,
the one who alone is immortal,
the one who lives in unapproachable light,
the one whom nobody has seen or can see:

You reveal yourself today in the face
of the little child of Bethlehem.

    Thanks to you, O Lord, thanks,
    forever!

John 1:1-18 1 Timothy 5:15-16.

TODAY THE WISE MEN COME TO BETHLEHEM

Glory and praise to you,
Lord Jesus Christ!

Today the Wise Men come to Bethlehem.
    With them, Lord,
we come to render homage to you.
Glory and praise to you, Lord Jesus Christ!

Today the star leads them to the manger.
    With them, Lord,
we wish to let ourselves be led by your light.
Glory and praise to you, Lord Jesus Christ!

Today they see the little child and Mary his mother.
    With them, Lord,
we wish to discover you in the midst of our brothers and sisters.
Glory and praise to you, Lord Jesus Christ!

Today they prostrate themselves before you and adore you.
    With them, Lord,
we wish to adore your holy will for us.
Glory and praise to you, Lord Jesus Christ!

Today they offer him their gifts.
    With them, Lord,
we wish to offer you our own lives as a gift.
Glory and praise to you, Lord Jesus Christ!

On this day [at this time] of your holy birth,
O Jesus Lord, we pray to you:
Let all our lives bring glory to you.
And because your birth was here on earth,
give us someday our own birth in heaven
    for one eternal Christmas.

YOUR STAR LED THE WISE MEN

Lord Jesus,
King of kings and Lord of lords,
infant born of the Virgin Mary,
your star led the Wise Men to the manger
and they paid homage to you in your mother's arms.
    We pray to you:

For each person, light this star —
a reason for hope and for love —
a star that rises in the heavens of our hearts
and leads to you.

Together with the Wise Men,
we can then offer you as gifts
the gold of our faithfulness,
the incense of our prayer,
and the myrrh of our sacrifice.

BLESSINGS FOR CHRISTMAS AND EPIPHANY

Glory to God in the highest
and peace to those who enjoy his favor!   —*Amen.*

May you be blest, God our Father!   —*Amen.*
The mystery kept secret for endless ages
you make known today to all nations
  through your Son Jesus Christ!   —*Amen.*
Glory to you forever!   —*Amen.*

Christ, visible in the flesh,   —*Amen.*
Christ, who was seen by the angels,   —*Amen.*
Christ, proclaimed among the nations.   —*Amen.*

See how God our Father has shown his love
  in his Son Jesus Christ
for the salvation of all people!   —*Amen.*
To him be glory forever!   —*Amen.*

  In this Christmas season
see how God manifests his goodness
and his love for all people
  in his Son Jesus Christ!   —*Amen.*
He saves us not because of our merits
  but according to his mercy.   —*Amen.*
To him be glory forever!   —*Amen.*

  Blest be God, our Lord!   —*Amen.*
After having spoken in the past to our fathers
  through the prophets,
he speaks to us in our own time through his Son,
  born for us of the Virgin Mary.   —*Amen.*

Each blessing concludes with the usual formula:

  May almighty God bless you,
  the Father, and the Son, and the Holy Spirit. Amen.

Luke 2:14   Romans 16:25-26   1 Timothy 3:16   Titus 2:11; 3:4-5   Hebrews 1:1-3.

LENT

AND

PASSIONTIDE

PRAYER OF THE EXODUS

Deliver us, O Lord!

Of old, you freed your people
    from the servitude of Egypt.
Liberate us today, we beg you,
    from the slavery of sin.

Of old, you fed your people in the desert
    with the manna from heaven.
Nourish us today, we beg you,
    with the bread of eternal life.

Of old, you gave your thirsty people
    the water springing from the rock.
Quench our thirst today, we beg you,
    with the water welling up to eternal life.

Of old, you gave your people at Sinai
    the commandments of the Covenant.
Give us today, we beg you,
    your grace and your truth.

Of old, you led your people in march
    by Moses, your servant.
Lead your Church today, we beg you,
    by Jesus Christ, your Son.

Of old, you opened to your people
    a door of hope in the promised land.
Open to us today, we beg you,
    the new heavens and the new earth.

Blessed are you, God our Father,
who calls us from this land of pain
to the homeland of your joy!

As your Son Jesus Christ
passed from this world to your reign,
he loved us to the end.
Teach us to imitate this perfect love
and, by his cross and passion,
to reach the promised land of his resurrection.

John 1:17; 4:14; 6:32-33; 10:1-16; 13:1.

PENITENTIAL LITANY

Gospel of Luke

With the publican of the Gospel, let us say:
O God, be merciful to me, a sinner!

You come to look for the lost sheep;
joyfully you carry it on your shoulders —
    we beg you:
O God, be merciful to me,
    a sinner!

You go to meet the prodigal son;
you clasp him in your arms and kiss him —
    we beg you:
O God, be merciful to me,
    a sinner!

You choose as your apostle Matthew the tax-collector;
you have not come to call the righteous, but sinners —
    we beg you:
O God, be merciful to me,
    a sinner!

You enter the house of Zachaeus the tax-collector
in order to seek out and save what was lost —
    we beg you:
O God, be merciful to me,
    a sinner!

You accept the ointment of the sinful woman;
because of her tears you pardon and defend her —
    we beg you:
O God, be merciful to me,
    a sinner!

To the good thief who implores you,
you open the gate of Paradise —
    we beg you:
O God, be merciful to me,
    a sinner!

Luke 5:27-32; 7:36-50; 15; 19:1-10; 23:39-43.

THE FAST THAT I LIKE, SAYS THE LORD

Help us to fast, O Lord, by loving one another.

"The fast that I like," says the Lord,
"is the breaking of the chains of evil,
the untying of the bonds of slavery."
        Help us to fast, O Lord,
        by loving our brothers and sisters.

"It is freeing the oppressed,
and welcoming the poor into your home."
        Help us to fast, O Lord,
        by loving our brothers and sisters.

"It is clothing the person you find naked,
and not despising your neighbor."
        Help us to fast, O Lord,
        by loving our brothers and sisters.

"Then will your light shine like the dawn,
and your wound be quickly healed over."
        Help us to fast, O Lord,
        by loving our brothers and sisters.

"Then, if you cry, God will answer;
if you call, he will say: I am here."
        Help us to fast, O Lord,
        by loving our brothers and sisters.

Isaiah 58:6-10.

I HAVE SPENT MY LIFE, LORD

Lord, have mercy.

I have spent my life, Lord,
tuning up my lyre
instead of singing to you.
    I am sorry, Lord.

I have spent my life, Lord,
looking for my own path
instead of walking with you.
    I am sorry, Lord.

I have spent my life, Lord,
begging for love
instead of loving you in my brothers and sisters.
    I am sorry, Lord.

I have spent my life, Lord,
fleeing the night
instead of saying: You are my light.
    I am sorry, Lord.

I have spent my life, Lord,
seeking security
instead of placing my hand in yours.
    I am sorry, Lord.

I have spent my life, Lord,
making resolutions
and not keeping them.
    I am sorry, Lord.

Now, if it is true, Lord,
that you save us
not because of our works
but because of your great mercy,
then we are now ready
to receive your salvation.

Ephesians 2:4-10.

BY ONE MAN'S DISOBEDIENCE

It is by the disobedience of one man,
    the first Adam,
that sin entered into the world,
and, through sin, death touches all of us.

It is by the obedience of one man also,
    Christ Jesus,
that we are led to the justice
    that gives life.

We pray to you, God our Father:
Since we all bear the wound of original sin,
let us also share in the original grace
    of Jesus, your Son.

Wherever our sin is multiplied,
let the grace of your Son abound.

CONSIDER OUR WEAKNESS, LORD

Consider our weakness, Lord!

The evil that we do not want,
    we do,
and the good that we desire,
    we do not do.

Accept the offering of our goodwill.
We ask you, Lord,
    not for victory without battle,
    not for peace without war,
but simply that you do not let us fight alone
and that we may be able to love you despite our weakness.

If your mercy is our strength,
then our battle will be your victory,
    in your Son Jesus Christ.

By One Man's Disobedience, *Romans 5:12-21,* First Sunday, A.
Consider Our Weakness, Lord, *Romans 7:14-20.*

THE TEMPTATION OF JESUS

Lead us not into temptation,
but deliver us from evil!

Lord Jesus, you told us:
"Not on bread alone is man to live
but on every utterance that comes from the mouth of God."
　We pray to you:
Help us during this season of Lent
to live more abundantly by your Word.
Help us also not to give into the temptation
of expecting a miracle to give us free bread
when we can earn it by our work.

Lead us not into temptation,
but deliver us from evil!

Then it was said to you:
"He will bid his angels take care of you;
with their hands they will support you
that you may never stumble on a stone."
　We pray to you:
Help us never to lack confidence in your protection.
Help us also not to fall into the temptation
of asking for the miraculous help of angels
when we ourselves can move the stones from our road.

Lead us not into temptation,
but deliver us from evil!

Also you told us:
"You shall do homage to the Lord your God;
him alone shall you adore."
　We pray to you:
Remove from our hearts the attraction of idols,
because you alone are our Lord and Master.
Help us also, in our adoration of you,
not to fall into the temptation
of forgetting to serve and help our brothers and sisters.

Lead us not into temptation,
but deliver us from evil!

Matthew 4:1-11, First Sunday, A.

Lord Jesus,
you have become like one of us,
you have suffered the test of temptation,
    we pray to you:
Be our merciful and faithful high priest,
come to the aid of those who fall,
    and deliver us from evil!

PRAYER TO THE TRANSFIGURED CHRIST

With Peter, James, and John,
lead us up on a high mountain
where we will be able to gaze upon you,
    O transfigured Christ!

With Moses and Elijah, your servants,
welcome us into your glory
and speak to us about your Father.

With the apostles, as you wake us from our dreams,
allow us to raise our eyes to you
and see you alone, Jesus.

O only Son, full of grace and truth,
allow us one day to hear
the voice of your Father saying to us from heaven,
"You too are my beloved sons
whom I have given all my love."

Then our lives will be transfigured
    in eternity.

The Temptation of Jesus, *Hebrews 2:17-18.*
Prayer to the Transfigured Christ, *Matthew 17:1-9 Mark 9:2-10 Luke 9:28-36,*
Second Sunday. *See also* Like Abraham, p. 262, Second Sunday, A, *and* The
Firstborn of Many, p. 248.

I WILL ANSWER HIM WHO CALLS UPON ME

To the one who loves you, Lord,
and who takes refuge under your wings,
　　　you promise in the psalm:

"He shall call upon me, and I will answer him;
I will be with him in distress...."

We pray to you: fulfill your promise.
Here we are in distress:
　　　stay by our side!
To you we cry:
　　　save us
through Jesus Christ, our Redeemer
　　　and our brother.

PRAYER FOR OUR BODIES

We pray to you, Lord, for our bodies.

　　　You have given them to us
to reveal ourselves to one another,
to communicate with our brothers and sisters,
to express our internal adoration of you.

Do not ever deprive us of them.
They are our earthly dwelling places:
transfigure them into eternal dwelling places
　　　on the day of your return.

They are our bodies of misery today:
transform them into images of your glorified body
　　　on the day of your resurrection.

They are disfigured by suffering and death:
dress them in the garment of your splendor
　　　for the feast of the new heavens
　　　and the new earth.

I Will Answer Him Who Calls upon Me, *Psalm 91:15,* First Sunday, C.
Prayer for Our Bodies, *2 Corinthians 5:1-4 Philippians 3:20-21,* Second
Sunday, C.

THE MAN BORN BLIND

Lord Jesus,
you opened the eyes of the man born blind,
you revealed yourself to him as Savior —
We, blindlike, extend our hands to you
    and pray:

Behold the shadows that descend on our minds:
    Enlighten us!
See how night falls in our hearts:
    Save us!

Send your Holy Spirit upon us.
May he illumine the eyes of our hearts
so that we also might recognize you
    as Savior!

May he bring the dawn of that eternal Day
when we shall see clearly
the love of your Father for each of us.

LISTEN, LORD

Listen to our prayer, Lord;
pardon our sins according to your love;
deliver us for the honor of your name.

Let the whole world know
that you are the Lord, our God,
and that we are the people who bear your name.

The Man Born Blind, *John 9 Ephesians 1:17-18 Isaiah 52:8,* Fourth Sunday, A.
See also "I Am," p. 231, Fourth Sunday, A, *and* The Seven Miracles of the Gospel
According to John, p. 206, Fourth Sunday.
Listen, Lord, *Baruch 2:14.*

YOU WHO DELIGHT IN SHOWING MERCY

Who is like you, Lord,
who always pardons sin,
who delights in showing mercy?

Once more have pity on us,
put down our faults,
throw them to the bottom of the sea!

Grant us your love and your fidelity
as you have promised to our fathers,
in the name of the love that you bear
toward your only Son, Jesus Christ,
our Savior and our brother.

FATHER OF JESUS

Father of Jesus, my brother and Savior:
    when I cry to you,
"My God, my God, why have you forsaken me?"
    do not reject me!
Recognize in my cry the voice of your Son,
and teach me to say with him,
"Father, into your hands I commend my spirit."

You Who Delight in Showing Mercy, *Micah 7:18-19.*
Father of Jesus, *Matthew 27:46 = Psalm 22:2, Luke 23:44 = Psalm 31:6.*

YOU WHO AWAIT THE RETURN OF THE SINNER

Blessed be you, O Lord, O Merciful One —
you who await the return of the sinner,
you who rejoice over finding the lost sheep,
you who embrace the son
    who returns to his home.

Bestow your mercy on all of us,
soften the hardness of our hearts,
break the pride of our impenitent spirits.

Do not close the door of your house, Lord!
Wait until the last of your children returns.
And only then begin for eternity
    the feast of your mercy!

THE TIME OF REPENTANCE

God of love,
you give your sons and daughters the fond hope
that, after sin, you leave room for repentance.

Give each of us the joy
of using this time of Lent
to return to you with all our hearts
as a child returns to his father.

You Who Await the Return of the Sinner, *Luke 15,* Fourth Sunday, C.
See also God Our Father, p. 266, Fourth Sunday, B, *and* Penitential Litany
According to Luke, p. 145, Fourth Sunday, C.
The Time of Repentance, *Wisdom 12:19.*

THE RESURRECTION OF LAZARUS

Lord Jesus,
you are the resurrection and the life.
Those who believe in you
will not die forever!
With Martha and Mary we implore you:
"Look! The one you love is ill,
he is near death!"

Lift from our hearts the sadness
that crushes them like a tombstone.
Tear from our faces the wrappings
that shroud them as garments of grief.

And when you weep at the sight of our distress
as you did at the grave of Lazarus,
we are filled with joy, Lord!
For then we know that your voice
will summon us to leave our graves
to live in the joy of your love
        forever!

OPEN OUR GRAVES

Open our graves, Lord,
remove us from the prison of death.

Place your Spirit in us
so that we may live
in a world of freedom.

The Resurrection of Lazarus, *John 11:1-45*, Fifth Sunday, A.
Open Our Graves, *Ezekiel 37:12-14*, Fifth Sunday, A.

LITANY OF THE PASSION

Have mercy, O Lord,
have mercy on us!

Lord Jesus,
in agony in the garden of Olives,
troubled by sadness and fear,
comforted by an angel:
Have mercy, O Lord, have mercy on us!

Lord Jesus,
betrayed by Judas' kiss,
abandoned by your apostles,
delivered into the hands of sinners:
Have mercy, O Lord, have mercy on us!

Lord Jesus,
accused by false witnesses,
condemned to die on the cross,
struck by servants, covered with spittle:
Have mercy, O Lord, have mercy on us!

Lord Jesus,
disowned by Peter, your apostle,
delivered to Pilate and Herod,
counted among the likes of Barabbas:
Have mercy, O Lord, have mercy on us!

Lord Jesus,
carrying your cross to Calvary,
consoled by the daughters of Jerusalem,
helped by Simon of Cyrene:
Have mercy, O Lord, have mercy on us!

Lord Jesus,
stripped of your clothes,
given vinegar to drink,
crucified with thieves:
Have mercy, O Lord, have mercy on us!

Lord Jesus,
insulted on the cross,
praying for your executioners,
pardoning the good thief:
Have mercy, O Lord, have mercy on us!

Lord Jesus,
entrusting your mother to your beloved disciple,
giving up your spirit into the hands of your Father,
dying for all of us sinners:
Have mercy, O Lord, have mercy on us!

By your sufferings, Lord,
heal the wounds in our hearts.
Let your tears be the source of joy for us,
and let your death give us life.

OUR GRIEF

Ah, Lord! Look at our grief!

Our life is like a dream
that disappears in the morning.
Our years unravel
like a garment that is wearing out.
And our thoughts are more wayward
than a ribbon of cloud
that wanders about the sky.

We humbly pray:
Give us the wisdom to number our days
not in months or years,
but simply according to how much
our love for you grows each day.

Our Grief, *Psalm 90:12* and *Psalm 102:27.*
See also Carry the Cross Each Day, p. 267.

BLESSINGS FOR THE LENTEN SEASON

May you be blessed, Lord Jesus,
who died for our sins
and rose again to give us life!   —*Amen.*
To you be glory forever!   —*Amen.*

The grace and peace of God our Father
        and the Lord Jesus Christ!   —*Amen.*
He sacrificed himself for our sins
to rescue us from this wicked world
        in accordance with the will of his Father.   —*Amen.*
To him be glory forever!   —*Amen.*

We give you thanks, our Father!
You call us to join with the saints
        and to inherit your light.   —*Amen.*
You take us out of the power of darkness
and create a place for us in the Kingdom
        of the Son of your love.   —*Amen.*
To you be glory forever!   —*Amen.*

May God grant us salvation
through our Lord Jesus Christ!   —*Amen.*
He died and arose from the dead for us,
so that, awake or asleep,
we might live together with him.   —*Amen.*

        May the God of peace,
who brought our Lord Jesus Christ back from the dead
        to become the great Shepherd of his sheep
        in the blood of a New Covenant,
help us to do his will in every kind of good deed.   —*Amen.*
May he realize in us whatever is acceptable to him
        through Jesus Christ!   —*Amen.*
To him be glory forever!   —*Amen.*

Blessed be the God and Father of our Lord Jesus Christ! —*Amen.*
In his great mercy he has given us a new birth
by raising Jesus Christ from the dead.
To him be glory forever!   —*Amen.*

Romans 4:25 Galatians 1:3-5 Colossians 1:12-13
1 Thessalonians 5:9-10 Hebrews 13:20-21 1 Peter 1:3.

May grace and peace be given us by Jesus Christ!
He is the faithful witness,
the firstborn from the dead,
the ruler of the kings of the earth.   —*Amen.*
He loves us and has washed away our sins with his blood.
He has made us a kingdom of priests
    for his God and Father.   —*Amen.*
To him be glory and power forever!   —*Amen.*

Each blessing concludes with the usual formula:

    May almighty God bless you,
    the Father, and the Son, and the Holy Spirit. Amen.

Revelation 1:5-7.

THE PASCHAL CYCLE

PROCLAIMING YOUR RESURRECTION

Jesus Christ, risen Lord,
have mercy on us!

Help us, O risen Lord,
to proclaim your resurrection,
by bringing good news to the poor
and healing the hearts that are broken.

Help us, O risen Lord,
to proclaim your resurrection,
by feeding those who are hungry
and clothing those who are naked.

Help us, O risen Lord,
to proclaim your resurrection,
by releasing the captives of injustice
and all those who are imprisoned by their sins.

Help us, O risen Lord,
to proclaim your resurrection,
by welcoming the strangers
and visiting those in loneliness.

Help us, O risen Lord,
to proclaim your resurrection,
by bringing your peace to those who are in trouble
and your joy to those who are in sorrow.

God our Father,
who raised your Son from the dead,
help us to understand, we beg you,
that we conquer our own death
and rise with Jesus today
when we live in love.

We ask you this grace through Jesus Christ,
who died for our sins
and rose for our life.

Isaiah 61:1-2   Matthew 25:31-40   Romans 4:25.

WE REMEMBER YOU, O RISEN LORD

Alleluia, Alleluia, Alleluia!

We remember you, O risen Lord,
firstborn of the dead.
Your resurrection destroys the power of death
and changes tears of agony into cries of joy.
> Blessed are you!

We remember you, O risen Lord,
new springtime in our life.
Your resurrection covers the fields with flowers
and brings the new creation into our hearts.
> Blessed are you!

We remember you, O risen Lord,
new Exodus from the land of sin.
Your resurrection gives us the signal
for a new departure in a life of grace.
> Blessed are you!

We remember you, O risen Lord,
new Moses on the mountain.
Your resurrection opens the gates
of the new heavens and the new earth.
> Blessed are you!

We remember you, O risen Lord,
Prophet of the messianic time.
Your resurrection initiates the law
of the new love with a renewed heart.
> Blessed are you!

We remember you, O risen Lord,
New Covenant at the feast of the cross.
Your resurrection dresses the table
for the bread of heaven and the cup of salvation.
> Blessed are you!

Luke 1:78   1 Corinthians 5:7   2 Timothy 1:10   Revelation 1:5; 21:1-5.

BY YOUR RESURRECTION

Alleluia, Alleluia, Alleluia!

By your resurrection, O Lord,
you become the firstborn of the dead.
Help us live the newness of your life.

By your resurrection
you seal the New Covenant.
Place in our hearts your own Spirit.

By your resurrection
you killed hate among people.
Help us live the new law of your love.

By your resurrection
you clothed yourself with immortality.
Help us put on the New Man
created in justice and holiness of truth.

By your resurrection
you sit at the right hand of your Father.
Help us discover in the earthly realities
the path to your heavenly Kingdom.

By your resurrection
you restore the universe.
Rebuild also your Church in your joy,
because the life of your risen people
is the witness of your resurrection.

Philippians 2:16　Ephesians 4:24　Colossians 3:1-2
Hebrews 8:7-13　Revelation 21:5.

THIS IS THE DAY YOU HAVE MADE FOR US

This is the day you have made for us,
  risen Lord,
a day of happiness and joy!

  We pray to you, Lord:
Make each day that you give us
the most beautiful day of our lives,
because it is the day you have chosen
for us to encounter you,
    O risen Christ!

YOUR RESURRECTION IS THE HOPE OF OUR OWN

May you be blessed, Lord Jesus,
because your resurrection is the hope of our own,
and the glory that will clothe us on the last day
is a reflection of that which clothed you
  on Easter morning.

  We pray to you:
Let all our lives express this hope
by their constant renewal through the joy of your love
  and the service of our brothers and sisters.

TO TESTIFY TO YOUR RESURRECTION

May you be blessed, Lord Jesus,
you who call us to testify to your resurrection
  unto the ends of the earth!
  But come to our aid,
so that our testimony may be worthy of you.

You wish us to proclaim that you are living,
though we ourselves fear death.

This Is the Day You Have Made for Us, *Psalm 118.*
Your Resurrection Is the Hope of Our Own, *Colossians 3:1-4.*

You wish us to announce your light,
though we grope in the darkness.

You command us to speak with authority,
though we stutter in ignorance before your mystery.

You wish us to affirm your free gift of mercy for all people,
though we have to beg for it, first of all, for ourselves.

You wish to make us God's assistants,
though we carry the weight of our own fatigue.

Can anything make so many contradictions work together
        except your love alone?
A love that calls us in spite of our faults,
that gives us confidence in spite of our unfaithfulness!

To you be glory, O wonderful Christ,
with the Father and the Holy Spirit,
        forever!

YOU RAISE US UP WITH CHRIST

May you be blessed, Lord, God our Father!

When we are dead because of our sins,
you give us new life with Christ;
with him you raise us up,
with him you make us reign in heaven.

We pray to you: help us to live from now on
no longer as strangers to the Kingdom,
but as people familiar with the house of God.

Let all our resurrected life announce
the love that you offer all people
and the joy with which you brighten all lives,
through your Son Jesus Christ,
who is our life and our resurrection
        forever.

Ephesians 2:5-6, 19.

MY LORD AND MY GOD!

Lord Jesus,
you appeared to your apostles after the resurrection
and filled their hearts with joy when you said to them,
    "Peace be with you!"

Come also into the midst of this community.
Bring it the peace of your presence,
and may your joy overflow our hearts
    like the springtime sun.
Then with your apostle Thomas we will greet you
    with a joyful shout:
      "My Lord and my God!"

VICTORY OVER THE WORLD

Lord Jesus, your apostle tells us:
"This is the victory over the world —
    our faith!"

    We pray to you:
Increase our faith
so that we might, first of all, triumph
    over our own unbelief.

Grant that our victory over the world
will be to serve those who do not believe.
Make our victory so beautifully humble
that they will wish to join us.
Let them also come to triumph over themselves
by becoming children of God
    through faith.

My Lord and My God! *John 20:19-20.*
Victory over the World, *1 John 5:1-6.*

UNITED HEART AND SOUL

Lord Jesus, your resurrection has brought together
the multitude of believers into a single community.
   We pray:

May your Church of today, like that of old,
      have but one heart,
      but one soul.

In the unity of its faith in you
and its love for its brothers and sisters,
may it bear witness to your resurrection
with the power of the Holy Spirit.

STAY WITH US, LORD

Walk with us, Lord,
along the road of resurrection!

Explain for us, so slow to believe,
the things that Scripture says of you.

Break the bread of the Eucharist with us
whenever we share our lives
      with our brothers and sisters.

      Stay with us
each time night approaches
and the daylight fades in our hearts!

United Heart and Soul,   *Acts 4:32-35.*
Stay with Us, Lord,   *Luke 24:13-15.*

IN EACH PAGE OF SCRIPTURE

Lord Jesus,
open our spirits to the understanding of the Scriptures
as you opened those of your apostles.
Explain to us what concerns you
in the Law of Moses, in the prophets and the psalms.

Then in each page of Scripture
we will be able to see your face,
     O risen Lord!

PUT HATRED TO DEATH

By your death, Lord Jesus, put hatred to death,
and by your resurrection, bring love back to life.

Reconcile all people with the Father;
bring together all nations
into a New Man;
destroy the barriers
that sin erects between people.

Proclaim peace to those who are far away,
and to those who are near.

Open the way of the Spirit to your Father,
you who are our life and our resurrection
     for all eternity.

In Each Page of Scripture, *Luke 24:44-45,* Third Sunday, B.
Put Hatred to Death, *Ephesians 2:14-18.*

THE GOOD SHEPHERD

Gather together your sheep, Lord,
in all the places where they have been scattered
during the mist and darkness.

Lead them to good pasturage;
let them rest in good grazing ground.

Those who are lost — search out;
those who have strayed — bring back.

Those who are wounded — bind their wounds;
those who are sick — cure.

Those bearing young — watch over them;
all of your sheep — keep them safe in your flock.

    Lord Jesus,
because you are our good shepherd,
help us all to be the sheep of your flock.

Gather all people into the fold of your love
so that there may be but one flock
    and one shepherd.

SUCH A SHEPHERD

Ever a shepherd who feeds his flock,
who carries the sheep in his arms,
who cradles them on his breast,
who leads the mother ewes to their rest —
such a shepherd are you for each of us, Lord.
    May you be blest
    forever and ever!

The Good Shepherd, *Ezekiel 34:11-16 Isaiah 40:10 John 10.*
Such a Shepherd, *Isaiah 40:10. See also* "I Am," p. 231.

WE SHALL COME TO HIM

Lord Jesus, you said:
"If anyone loves me,
he will keep my Word,
and my Father will love him;
and we shall come to him
and make our home with him."
    We pray:

Look at our misery.
We have not been faithful to the Word,
yet we dare to ask you:
    Do not abandon us,
but come make your home with us
    not because of our merits
but simply because you are merciful.

GREATER THAN OUR HEARTS

Lord Jesus,
sometimes our hearts reproach us.
But you are greater than our hearts!

Your pardon is greater than our weakness;
your joy lessens our anguish,
and your strength overcomes our distress.

Keep us in the assurance of your love
and our hearts will remain at peace.

We Shall Come to Him, *John 14:23-24*, Fifth Sunday, A.
Greater than Our Hearts, *1 John 3:19-20*, Fifth Sunday, B.
See also "I Am Going to Prepare a Place for You," p. 266, *and* Source of All
Joy, p. 250.

THE HOPE THAT IS IN US

God our Father, you wish us
always to be ready to answer
anyone who asks the reason
for the hope that is in us.

We pray to you:
Place in us your Holy Spirit,
the Spirit of truth and love.

Help us to bear witness to your truth
        with the purest charity,
so that our truth may always be charitable,
full of respect for those who do not believe.

Help us also to bear witness to your love
        with a shining truth,
so that our love may always be true,
full of patience for those who do not love you.

Then we will be witnesses of your Son Jesus,
in whom love and truth dwell together.

A NEW LIFE

By your death, Lord Jesus,
make the old man die in us,
and by your resurrection,
clothe us again with the New Man,
created for holiness and truth.

Help us to abandon forever
        the oldness of sin,
so that, from now on, we will have a new life
        in the joy of your resurrection.

The Hope That Is in Us, *1 Peter 3:15-18,* Sixth Sunday, A.
A New Life, *Ephesians 4:24.*

THE ASCENSION

Jesus Christ,
Lord glorified on high,
look with love upon your brothers and sisters on earth.

Your ascension is the hope
of our future glory,
and your presence near your Father
announces our own entrance into the eternal dwelling.

We pray to you:
Let the desire for heavenly realities
not make us neglect our work on earth.

Let our hope for the future
inspire in us a respect for the present moment.

Let your ascension into heaven move us
to make your glory dwell on earth.

Thus we will be witnesses to your presence
among our brothers and sisters
until the end of time.

Acts 1:8   Ephesians 2:6.

NEAR HIM IN YOUR KINGDOM

God our Father,
you who have raised your Son Jesus Christ
   from among the dead,
   we pray to you:

Raise us with him;
place us near him in your Kingdom.

Allow us to carry in our bodies
the suffering and death of Jesus
so that the life itself of Jesus
may always be seen in our mortal flesh.

And when our earthly dwelling is destroyed,
give us the everlasting home
that was not built by human hands
but that your love has built for us
   in heaven.

We ask this of you through your Son Jesus Christ,
him who is our life and our resurrection,
in the love of the Holy Spirit,
   forever.

WE PASS FROM DEATH TO LIFE

We know that we pass
   from death to life
when we love our brothers and sisters.

Grant us, then, Lord Jesus,
   from this very moment
to rise from the dead with you
   by loving our brothers and sisters
   as you love us.

Near Him in Your Kingdom, *2 Corinthians 4:10-14; 5:1 John 11:25.*
We Pass from Death to Life, *1 John 3:14.*

BLESSINGS FOR THE EASTER SEASON

May you be blessed, Lord Jesus,
who died for our sins
and rose again for our life!   —*Amen.*
To you be glory forever!   —*Amen.*

Let us give thanks to God, who gives us victory
through our Lord Jesus Christ!   —*Amen.*

Blessed be God our Father,
who raised his Son Jesus Christ to life!   —*Amen.*
He will raise us one day with him
and will place us together by his side!   —*Amen.*

May God grant us salvation
through our Lord Jesus Christ!   —*Amen.*
He died and arose from the dead for us
so that, awake or asleep,
we might live together with him.   —*Amen.*
To him be glory forever!   —*Amen.*

Jesus Christ: the same,
yesterday, today, and forever.   —*Amen.*
To him be glory and honor
forever and ever.   —*Amen.*

May the God of peace
who brought our Lord Jesus Christ back from the dead
to become the great Shepherd of the sheep
in the blood of a New Covenant,
help us to do his will in every kind of work.   —*Amen.*
May he realize in us everything that is pleasing to him,
through Jesus Christ!   —*Amen.*
To him be glory forever!   —*Amen.*

Blessed be the God and Father of our Lord Jesus Christ!   —*Amen.*
In his great mercy, he has given us a new birth
by raising Jesus Christ from the dead.   —*Amen.*

Romans 4:25   1 Corinthians 15:57   2 Corinthians 4:14
1 Thessalonians 5:9-10   Hebrews 13:8, 20-21   1 Peter 1:3.

May grace and peace be given us by Jesus Christ!   —*Amen.*
He is the faithful witness,
the firstborn from the dead,
the ruler of the kings of the earth.   —*Amen.*
He loves us and redeems us from our sins by his blood.
He makes us a kingdom of priests
     for his God and Father.   —*Amen.*
To him be glory and power forever!   —*Amen.*

Each blessing concludes with the usual formula:

    May almighty God bless you,
    the Father, and the Son, and the Holy Spirit. Amen.

Revelation 1:5-7.

PENTECOST

AND

THE CHURCH

POUR OUT YOUR SPIRIT, LORD

POUR OUT YOUR SPIRIT, LORD, ON ALL HUMANKIND,
AS YOU DID ON THE FIRST PENTECOST!

POUR OUT YOUR SPIRIT ON OUR SONS AND OUR DAUGHTERS,
ON THE YOUNG AND THE OLD,
ON THE SLAVES AND THE SERVANTS,
ON THE MEN AND THE WOMEN!

MAY ALL OF US BECOME A PROPHETIC PEOPLE,
    THE PEOPLE OF JESUS!

Joel 3:1-2 Acts 2:17-18.

THE HOLY SPIRIT AND PENTECOST

The following liturgical prayers ask for the grace of the Holy Spirit.

The first recalls certain traditional elements that concern the theology of the gifts of the Holy Spirit and that are found in Isaiah 11:2 and in Galatians 5:22-23.

The second has, as its source, the texts of Scripture which manifest the presence of the Spirit in the life of Jesus.

The third uses the scriptural texts that reflect the presence of the Spirit in the ancient community as recorded in the Acts of the Apostles.

The fourth prayer, the longest of all, recalls the texts that refer to the action of the Holy Spirit according to other scriptural sources, most particularly the Epistles of St. Paul.

It is evident, however, that one must choose from among the many suggested intentions of these prayers, and that those chosen should be adapted not only to the quality of the celebrating assembly but also to the rite of the celebration. Therefore, in an ordinary celebration, it would be better to engage the attention of the assembly by moderation than by excess. Thus three or four well-chosen intentions quietly and fervently presented would serve as a greater aid to prayer than would eight or ten made with haste or thoughtlessness.

In regard to the President's Oration that concludes these prayers, it is better that it be addressed to the Father. It is the Father, in effect, who, through the Son, gives us the Holy Spirit, and it is the Spirit of Jesus Christ who leads us to the Father, the first source of all holiness, of all love, and of all joy.

For these four prayers the following responses are suggested: *Come to us, Holy Spirit! — Come to us, Spirit of Holiness! — Come to us, Spirit of the Lord!*

THE SPIRIT TOO HELPS US IN OUR WEAKNESS,
FOR WE DO NOT KNOW HOW TO PRAY AS WE OUGHT:
BUT THE SPIRIT HIMSELF MAKES INTERCESSION FOR US
WITH GROANINGS THAT CANNOT BE EXPRESSED
IN SPEECH.

Romans 8:26.

THE GIFTS OF THE SPIRIT

Let us pray to the Lord Jesus
that he place in us
the gifts of his Spirit
and the power of his love.
>*Come to us, Spirit of the Lord!*

Spirit of wisdom,
Spirit of understanding,
Spirit of adoration,
>Come to us, Spirit of the Lord!

Spirit of strength,
Spirit of knowledge,
Spirit of joy,
>Come to us, Spirit of the Lord!

Spirit of love,
Spirit of peace,
Spirit of jubilation,
>Come to us, Spirit of the Lord!

Spirit of willing service,
Spirit of goodness,
Spirit of gentleness,
>Come to us, Spirit of the Lord!

God our Father,
source of all love and joy,
you who never measure the grace of your Spirit
but offer it to every person
with the royal generosity of divine giving,
>we pray to you:

In giving us the Spirit of your Son,
pour into our hearts the fullness of love,
so that we are able to love you alone
yet preserve all our tenderness for people also,
>in this unique love,
>through Christ our Lord.
>Amen.

Isaiah 11:2 Galatians 5:22-23 John 3:34 Romans 5:5.

THE SPIRIT IN THE LIFE OF JESUS

Holy Spirit,
who came upon the Virgin Mary
so that she became the Mother of Jesus,   *Lk 1:34*
    we pray to you:
Open our hearts to your word,
help us to receive Jesus, the Word of God.

Holy Spirit,
who came upon Zechariah, Elizabeth, and Simeon,   *Lk 1:41, 67*
and helped them recognize the Messiah,   *Lk 2:26*
    we pray to you:
Enlighten the eyes of our hearts
so that we may know how to recognize Jesus, the Lord.

Holy Spirit,   *Mt 3:16*
who came upon Christ Jesus   *Mk 1:10*
when he was baptized in the waters of the Jordan,   *Lk 3:22*
    we pray to you:
Baptize us in the fire of your love
so that the Father may say to each of us: *Mt 3:17*
"You are my beloved Son.   *Lk 3:22*
On you my favor rests."

Holy Spirit,   *Mt 4:1*
who led Christ Jesus   *Mk 1:12*
out into the desert of temptation,   *Lk 4:1*
    we pray to you:
Give us the strength
to conquer in ourselves the power of evil.

Holy Spirit,
who sent Christ Jesus   *Mt 12:18-21*
to carry the Good News to the poor,   *Lk 4:18-19*
    we pray to you:
Help us to continue your work
by serving the poor, our brothers and sisters.

Holy Spirit,
who filled Christ Jesus with joy   *Lk 10:21*
and opened his mouth to praise the Father,   *Mt 11:27*
    we pray to you:
Teach us to say to him,
"Yes, Father, your gracious will be done!"

Holy Spirit,
you who speak through the mouth of despised disciples,
    we pray to you: *Mt 10:20*
Place in us your words of wisdom;   *Lk 13:11*
help us to conquer evil by good.   *Rom 12:21*

Holy Spirit,
in whom Jesus, the perfect oblation,
is offered to the love of his Father,   *Heb 9:14*
    we pray to you:
Make of us an eternal offering
in praise of your glory.   *Eph 1:14*

THE SPIRIT IN THE ACTS OF THE APOSTLES

> Let us call upon the Spirit of Jesus:
> Today, as in the time of the apostles,
> may he assist his Church
> for the glory of God the Father.

Spirit of Jesus,
poured out in flames of fire upon your disciples   *Acts 2:1-11*
on the day of Pentecost,   *(4:31)*
    we pray to you:
Set afire the hearts of your faithful
so that they will announce in all the languages of the world
the wonders of the salvation of God.

Holy Spirit,
who helped Peter before the Sanhedrin   *Acts 4:8*
when he gave testimony to Christ Jesus,
    we pray to you:
Help us to announce with confidence   *Acts 5:32*
the Good News of Jesus Christ.

Holy Spirit,
who filled Stephen the martyr with your wisdom,
who opened the heavens before him   *Acts 6:10*
and showed him Jesus
standing at the right hand of his Father,   *Acts 7:55*
    we pray to you:
Enlighten the eyes of our hearts
so that in the difficulties
and the persecutions of this world
we may know how to recognize the presence of the Lord.

Holy Spirit,
who led the deacon Philip on the road from Gaza
to the meeting with the eunuch of the queen of Ethiopia
and had him announce the Good News of Jesus,
    we pray to you: *Acts 8:26-40*
Lead your missionaries
toward all those who are seeking the truth.

Holy Spirit,
who built up the infant churches   *Acts 9:31*
and filled them with your consolation,
    we pray to you:
Make the Kingdom of God on earth
grow by your joy and your peace.

Holy Spirit,
who called Paul and Barnabas
to their mission among the pagans   *Acts 13:4*
and filled them with the joy
of announcing the Good News,   *Acts 13:52*
    we pray to you:
Today again bring to life some fervent witnesses for Christ.

Holy Spirit,
who helped the apostles at the council of Jerusalem
and inspired their decisions,   *Acts 15:28*
    we pray to you:
Enlighten those in authority
that their ministry
will be of service to their brothers and sisters.   *Acts 20:28*

Holy Spirit,
you who pointed out the way for your disciples
to announce the Gospel,   *Acts 16:6-8*
    we pray to you:
As in the time of the apostles,
guide today's messengers of the Good News.

COME TO US, SPIRIT OF HOLINESS

The Spirit in the Epistles

Let us humbly call upon the Holy Spirit
so that our life in Christ Jesus
may glorify God our Father.

Spirit of Jesus,
you pour the love of God into our hearts;   *Rom 5:5*
    we pray to you:
Enflame all our lives
with the fire of your love.

Spirit of Jesus,
you help us to serve God our Father
in the new life of the Spirit
and not in the oldness of the letter;   *Rom 7:6*
    we pray to you:
When we read the Word of God,
lift the veil from our hearts   *2 Cor 3:14*
so that we will discover there the face of Jesus Christ.

Holy Spirit,
your law gives us life in Christ Jesus;   *Rom 8:3*
    we pray to you:
Free us from the law of sin and death.

Holy Spirit,
you raised Christ Jesus from the dead;   *Rom 8:11*
    we pray to you:
Stamp upon us the seal of eternal life.

Holy Spirit,
you banish fear from our hearts;
you bear witness in us that we are children of God;
    we pray to you:
Remove from our hearts the spirit of slaves;
place in us the spirit of adopted children   *Rom 8:15-17*
to make us cry out, "Abba, Father!"   *Gal 4:4*

Holy Spirit,
you come to the aid of our weakness
because we do not know how to pray as we should;   *Rom 8:26-27*
    we beg you:
Intercede for us,
and place in our hearts and on our lips
a prayer pleasing to the Father.

Spirit of Jesus,
you who are our life,   *Gal 5:25*
    we pray to you:
Help us to act as children of God
who follow Christ Jesus,
the firstborn of many brothers and sisters.   *Rom 8:29*

Spirit of Jesus,
you sanctified the pagans,
making them a pleasing offering to the Father;
    we pray to you:
Make us apostles of your Gospel,
ministers of Jesus Christ to the nations.   *Rom 15:16*

Holy Spirit,
you know the infinite depths of God;   *1 Cor 2:10-12*
    we pray to you:
Reveal to us the mystery of the Father
and the love that surpasses all knowledge.   *Eph 3:19*

Spirit of Jesus,
you make us holy temples
to the glory of the Father;
    we pray to you:
Help us to glorify God in our bodies.   *1 Cor 6:19-20*

Holy Spirit,
by your grace we can say:
"Jesus is Lord!"   *1 Cor 12:3*
Help us to live in holiness
and thus to proclaim the kingdom of Christ Jesus.

Holy Spirit,
you distribute your gifts
for the common good of the whole Church;   *1 Cor 12:4-11*
    we pray to you:
Let the variety of gifts and of ministries
strengthen the unity of the whole body
that everyone may be loved in the Church
for the special work he accomplishes.

Holy Spirit,
in you we have been baptized
to form only one Body;   *1 Cor 12:13*
    we pray to you:

Gather together all Christians
in the unity of your Church.

Holy Spirit,
pledge of our inheritance,   *2 Cor 1:22; 5:5*
you set your seal on our hearts;   *Eph 1:14*
    we pray to you:
Against the day of our redemption   *Eph 4:30*
seal us with the sign of Christ.

Spirit of Jesus,
wherever you reign,   *2 Cor 3:17*
there freedom triumphs;
    we pray to you:
Lead us to the complete truth,   *Jn 16:13*
so that your truth will make us free.   *Jn 8:32*

Holy Spirit,
you unite the Church in the bond of peace;   *Eph 4:3*
    we pray to you:
End all divisions in the Body of Christ,
gather us together in your love.

Spirit of God, Spirit of glory,
you come to rest on those who are insulted   *1 Pt 4:14*
for the name of Christ Jesus;
    we pray to you:
Fill with your strength and your peace
those who suffer persecution for the Kingdom.

Spirit of truth,   *Jn 14:17*
whom the Father sends in the name of the Son,
    we pray to you:
Recall to our memories the words of Jesus
and keep them in our hearts.   *Jn 14:26*

SANCTIFY YOUR GREAT NAME

Come to us, Spirit of the Lord!

Sanctify your great name
that our life has profaned.
Come to us, Spirit of the Lord!

Show your holiness
so that the world will recognize you as God.
Come to us, Spirit of the Lord!

Gather together your children
whom sin has scattered.
Come to us, Spirit of the Lord!

Pour clean water on us;
cleanse us of all our idols.
Come to us, Spirit of the Lord!

Remove our hearts of stone;
give us new hearts.
Come to us, Spirit of the Lord!

Pour your Spirit into us
so that we will walk according to your will.
Come to us, Spirit of the Lord!

You are our God, Lord:
Make us be your people!
Come to us, Spirit of the Lord!

Ezekiel 36:23-27.

YOUR SPIRIT, LORD, IS TRUTH

Come to us, Spirit of the Lord!

Your Spirit, Lord, is truth:
May it make us free.
Come to us, Spirit of the Lord!

Your Spirit, Lord, is fire:
May it enkindle us with love.
Come to us, Spirit of the Lord!

Your Spirit, Lord, is gentleness:
May it bring us peace.
Come to us, Spirit of the Lord!

Your Spirit, Lord, renews the face of the earth:
May it renew the depths of our hearts.
Come to us, Spirit of the Lord!

Your Spirit, Lord, is prayer:
May it open our hearts to give praise.
Come to us, Spirit of the Lord!

Your Spirit, Lord, fills the whole universe:
May it live among us forever.
Come to us, Spirit of the Lord!

Your Spirit, Lord, is life:
May it raise us up on the last day.
Come to us, Spirit of the Lord!

FOR THE CHURCH OF YOUR SON JESUS

God our Father, we pray to you
for the Church of your Son Jesus.

Let her be resplendent
with the beauty of Jesus;
let her avoid painting herself
with the vain beauty of the world.

Let her not be disfigured
by the wrinkles of old age;
let her represent for all people
the hope of the future.

Let her face be purified
from every stain of pride;
let her show preference
for the poor and the humble.

Let her be holy and spotless;
let her not be maimed by error.

Let her be beautiful as one betrothed,
all dressed up for her spouse;
let her shun the unseemly "adornments"
of money and power.

Lord Jesus,
you have loved your Church,
and you have given yourself up for her;
    we pray to you:
Guide this Church that she, in turn,
will love all people
and put herself at their service.

Ephesians 5:25-27.

LET HER REMOVE HER DRESS OF SORROW

We pray to you, God our Father,
for the Church of your Son Jesus.

May she remove her dress of sorrow;
may she put on the mantle of your justice;
may the crown of your glory sparkle on her head!

May her face shine
with the very splendor of the beauty of your Son!

In her journey toward you,
give her as escort, Lord,
your mercy and your justice.

THE TOTTERING HUT OF DAVID

Lord, God of our fathers,
you who have promised by the mouth of your prophet Amos:
"I will raise up the fallen hut of David,
wall up its breaches,
raise up its ruins,
and rebuild it as in the days of old,"
      we beg you:

See our Church that ruin threatens.
Wall up the breaches of its faults;
raise up the ruins of its love;
rebuild its faith on the rock of your Word.

Make it resplendent with the very beauty of Jesus
so that all people, tempted by its splendor,
will seek again and find in it the salvation and the joy
      of your Son Jesus Christ.

Let Her Remove Her Dress of Sorrow, *Baruch 5:1-9.*
The Tottering Hut of David, *Amos 9:11.*

GOD THE FATHER, SON, AND HOLY SPIRIT

Blest are you, O Lord,
through eternity!

God the Father,
we praise you and we bless you
because you are the Father of Jesus,
and because you wish to be our Father also
according to your love and mercy.
Blest are you, O Lord, through eternity!

God the Son,
we praise you and we bless you
because you are the Son of the Father's love,
and because you wish to be the eldest brother also
of all the children of God.
Blest are you, O Lord, through eternity!

God the Holy Spirit,
we praise you and we bless you
because you are the love of the Father and the Son,
springing up like a fire out of their affection,
and because you wish to dwell in our hearts also
like a furnace of love.
Blest are you, O Lord, through eternity!

God the Father, Son, and Holy Spirit,
we praise you and we bless you
because you are God surpassing all praise,
yet you accept the stammering
    of our adoration.
To you we direct our love forever and ever.
Blest are you, O Lord, through eternity!

BLESSED AMONG WOMEN BE THE VIRGIN MARY!
BLESSED IS JESUS, THE FRUIT OF HER LOVE!

HOLY MARY

WITH THE VIRGIN MARY

With the Virgin Mary,
our souls proclaim the greatness of the Lord
and our spirits exult with joy
in Jesus our Savior.
> *Blest are you, O Lord,*
> *through eternity!*

Because you have looked with favor
upon your lowly handmaid,
> blest are you, O Lord,
> through eternity!

Because the power of your love
has done great things for her,
> blest are you, O Lord,
> through eternity!

Because your mercy reaches from age to age
to all who worship you,
> blest are you, O Lord,
> through eternity!

Because you show the power of your arm
and scatter the proud of heart,
> blest are you, O Lord,
> through eternity!

Because you cast down princes from their thrones
and exalt the lowly,
> blest are you, O Lord,
> through eternity!

Because you fill the hungry with good things
and send the rich away empty,
> blest are you, O Lord,
> through eternity!

Because you are mindful of the mercy
promised to our fathers,
to Abraham and to his descendants forever,
> blest are you, O Lord,
> through eternity!

Luke 1:46-55.

We pray to you, God our Father:
Give us souls of praise
like that of the Virgin Mary,
souls that know how to marvel at your love
and find joy in telling you, "Thanks!"

JOY TO YOU, O VIRGIN MARY

Joy to you, O Virgin Mary,
Mother of the Lord!

Humble maiden of Nazareth,
betrothed to the carpenter Joseph,
greeted by the angel Gabriel!

Lowly handmaid of the Lord,
you on whom his favor rested,
to whom, all full of grace, the Lord was present!

Lovely Mother of Abraham's Son,
exalted Mother of David's Son,
Holy Mother of Jesus the Lord!

You most blessed among all women,
of whose own womb the fruit was blessed,
you most praised by all generations!

You to whom God's Holy Spirit came,
in whom the Word became our flesh,
through whose grace he dwells among us!

You who bore your Son, laid in a manger,
while angels sang "To God on high be glory,
and peace on earth to people of goodwill!"

You whose Child was sung to by the angels,
and acclaimed in joy by the shepherds,
as you marvelled at his wondrous birth!

You who showed him to the Wise Men,
you who brought him to the temple,
you who gave joy to aged Simeon!

Chosen Mother of the Messiah,
virgin and daughter of Sion,
glory and honor of God's holy people!

Suffering Mother under the cross,
glorious Mother of the apostles,
Queen and joy of all generations!

Glorious woman clothed with the sun,
with the moon under your feet,
on your head a crown of twelve stars!

WE GREET YOU, VIRGIN MARY

We greet you, Virgin Mary,
and we bless Jesus your Child.
To him be honor and praise
       Eternally!

Holy Mary,
Holy Mother of God,
Virgin full of grace,
Pray to the Lord for us.

Mother of Christ,
Mother of divine grace,
Mother most pure,
Pray to the Lord for us.

Mother ever Virgin,
Mother worthy of love,
Admirable Mother,
Pray to the Lord for us.

Mother of good counsel,
Mother of the Creator,
Mother of our Savior,
Pray to the Lord for us.

Faithful Virgin,
Mirror of holiness,
Throne of wisdom,
Pray to the Lord for us.

Source of our joy,
Abode of the Holy Spirit,
Mystical rose,
Pray to the Lord for us.

Ark of the Covenant,
Gate of Heaven,
Morning Star,
Pray to the Lord for us.

Consolation of the afflicted,
Refuge of sinners,
Strength of Christians,
Pray to the Lord for us.

Queen of angels,
Queen of patriarchs and prophets,
Queen of apostles,
Pray to the Lord for us.

Queen of martyrs,
Queen of virgins,
Queen of all saints,
Pray to the Lord for us.

Queen conceived without sin,
Queen raised up to heaven,
Queen of peace,
Pray to the Lord for us.

Lord Jesus, Son of the Virgin Mary,
you wished that all ages
proclaim your blessed Mother.

We also wish to fulfill the prophecy
and sing the glories of your Mother.

As praise, accept our lives,
offered in the service of our brothers and sisters,
     through love for you,
Jesus, Son of Mary and our brother.

ANNUNCIATION

We bless you, God our Father,
for having loved the Virgin Mary so much.

Through her we too find favor with you
    in her Son Jesus,
who today becomes our brother.

Send down upon us your Holy Spirit
so that we too might become the temple of your glory
and that Jesus might be born in our hearts
    through faith.

For nothing is impossible for your love.

VISITATION

Blest be the Virgin Mary among women!
Blest be Jesus, her Child!
Supremely blest is God our Father,
source of all grace and all blessing!

When Mary visited her cousin Elizabeth,
she brought her the presence of Jesus,
and was for her the source of joy.

Each time that we meet our brothers and sisters,
we can likewise bring them
    the presence of Jesus Christ
and enlighten them by the radiance of his joy.

God our Father, give us the same grace
that you bestowed through the Virgin Mary
on the day of the Visitation.
We ask this of you in the name of the love
that you have for your only Son, Jesus Christ,
and in memory of his beloved Mother.

Luke 1:26-38, 39-56.

PRESENTATION OF JESUS IN THE TEMPLE

Eternal God, born a tiny child,
you were presented in the temple in the arms of Mary,
and the aged Simeon proclaimed you
light of the nations and glory of your people Israel.

Through the hands of Mary, our sister,
we present you once again, today, to your Father.

Make your light rise
like a joyous dawn upon all those
    who do not know your name.
Be the glory of Israel, your people according to the flesh,
    who still have not recognized you.

And when the evening of our life arrives,
give us a share in Simeon's joy
at being able to see you in the peace of eternity.

ASSUMPTION

Lord Jesus, Son of the Virgin Mary,
we praise you and bless you
for having so glorified your Mother
in her soul and body.

If the day of death
is the day of birth into heaven,
your Mother was never so young
as on the morning of her Assumption.

Help us to grow old as she did
while continually becoming younger,
until the day when we will be children enough
to enter the Kingdom.

We ask this of you
in the name of the love you have for your Mother,
who is also our Mother
and the first of all the children of God.

Luke 2:22-40.

HANDMAID AND QUEEN

God our Father,
we praise you and give you thanks
for choosing the Virgin Mary
to be the Mother of your Son.

In her, the Word found a servant:
your love makes her a queen.

We pray to you:
Make us follow her as an example
that we might listen to your Word
and put it into practice.

May we then be able to share
the inheritance of eternal joy
that you give us
through your only Son Jesus Christ,
our Savior and our brother.

BLESSED BE THE LORD

Blessed be the Lord,
God and Father of our Lord Jesus Christ.

You have chosen the Virgin Mary
to be the Mother of your Son,
and you wish all ages to proclaim her blessed —
     we pray to you:

Because she learned to love us
by loving her firstborn Son,
help us serve you better
by singing her praises.

Enlarge the hearts of all people
so that they may recognize themselves
as brothers and sisters
and adore her Son, Jesus Christ, our Lord.

Luke 1:38, 42, 48.

PRAYERS
FOR
ALL SEASONS

YOU HAVE CREATED OUR BODIES

*Blest are you, O Lord,
through eternity!*

Blessed are you, Lord,
for the body of the child
that springs from the heart of its mother
    like a rosebud.

Blessed are you, Lord,
for the body of the young maiden
that you have clothed in grace and symmetry
and that is as beautiful as your betrothed,
    the Church.

Blessed are you, Lord,
for the bodies of husband and wife
who, in a harmony of flesh,
    speak their love to each other.

Blessed are you, Lord,
for the body of the celibate religious,
who spends all the strength of his love
    in the service of the Kingdom.

Blessed are you, Lord,
for the body of the old man or woman
whose timeworn face already bears the imprint
    of a joy that is more than earthly.

Blessed are you, Lord,
for the disfigured body of one who is dying,
whose moans are not so much from agony
    as from pains of being born into heaven.

Blessed are you, Lord,
for the beauty of our human bodies,
especially for the most beautiful of all,
that of your Mother, the Virgin Mary,
"the most blessed of all women,"
illuminated by the light and the splendor of heaven
    on the morning of her Assumption.

Blessed are you, Lord,
for your own body!

As a man of sorrows without brightness or beauty,
you were bruised by your sufferings on the cross
yet exalted by your Father in the glory of heaven.
Blessed are you who give us your risen body
as bread from heaven at the feast of the Covenant!

A PRAYER OF RENEWAL

Jesus Christ, risen Lord,
have mercy on us!

Lord Jesus, by your resurrection,
you renew the universe;
you change our death into your life;
　　　we pray to you:
Jesus Christ, risen Lord, have mercy on us!

Give us kindness wherever you find bitterness,
confidence wherever you find distress,
joy wherever you find sorrow;
　　　we pray to you:
Jesus Christ, risen Lord, have mercy on us!

Give us humility wherever pride reigns,
pardon wherever offense abides,
grace wherever sin abounds;
　　　we pray to you:
Jesus Christ, risen Lord, have mercy on us!

Give us love wherever hatred burns,
hope wherever despair is crying,
faith wherever doubt prevails;
　　　we pray to you:
Jesus Christ, risen Lord, have mercy on us!

Give us a new spirit in our old age,
a new heart to replace a heart of stone,
and the New Covenant in your holy resurrection;
　　　we pray to you:
Jesus Christ, risen Lord, have mercy on us!

WITH THEM WE PRAY TO YOU

Save us, O Lord, in the name of your love!

Lord Jesus,
you cleansed the leper.
With him we pray to you:
"Lord, if you wish,
heal us!"
Save us, O Lord, in the name of your love!

Lord Jesus,
you cured the centurion's servant.
With him we pray to you:
"Only say the word
and we shall be cured!"
Save us, O Lord, in the name of your love!

Lord Jesus,
you calmed the storm and saved the apostles.
With them we pray to you:
"Lord, save us!
Without you we perish."
Save us, O Lord, in the name of your love!

Lord Jesus,
you walked on the waters.
With Peter we pray to you:
"Lord, save us!
You are the Son of God."
Save us, O Lord, in the name of your love!

Lord Jesus,
you answered the Canaanite woman's request
to cure her daughter.
With her we pray to you:
"Lord, come and help us.
Give us the bread of children!"
Save us, O Lord, in the name of your love!

Lord Jesus,
you raised the daughter of Jairus.
With her father we pray to you:
"Lay your hand upon us,
and we will be saved and live!"
Save us, O Lord, in the name of your love!

Lord Jesus,
you cured the blind Bartimaeus
on the road to Jericho.
With him we pray to you:
"Jesus, Son of David,
have pity on us."
Save us, O Lord, in the name of your love!

Lord Jesus,
you pardoned the good thief on the cross.
With him we pray to you:
"Jesus, remember us
in your Kingdom!"
Save us, O Lord, in the name of your love!

Jesus Christ,
God of all tenderness
and Lord of all mercy,
you who spent your time on earth doing good,
    we pray to you:
Give to each of us our share of joy and happiness,
so that we can, on the road of life,
discover your love constantly,
bless and glorify you,
and arrive at perfect joy,
which is to live near your Father,
with you and the Holy Spirit,
forever and ever.
    Amen!

Matthew 8:1-4, 5-13, 23-27; 14:22-33; 15:21-28
Mark 5:21-43; 10:46 Luke 23:39-43 Acts 10:48.

THE SEVEN MIRACLES OF THE GOSPEL

According to the Gospel of John

Save us, O Lord, in the name of your love!

Lord Jesus,
at Cana in Galilee you changed water into wine.
    We pray to you:
Change to joy the sorrows of our earthly families
to show your glory to the world.
Save us, O Lord, in the name of your love!

Lord Jesus,
at Capernaum you restored to life
the dead son of a royal officer.
    We pray to you:
Revive our faith in the power of your Word
that saves us from death.
Save us, O Lord, in the name of your love!

Lord Jesus,
at the pool of Bethesda you cured a paralytic.
    We pray to you:
Deliver us from the paralysis of sin
and help us to walk with you.
Save us, O Lord, in the name of your love!

Lord Jesus,
in the desert you fed a hungry crowd
with five barley loaves and two fish.
    We pray to you:
Give each person the bread of both earth and heaven
and satisfy our hunger for eternity.
Save us, O Lord, in the name of your love!

Lord Jesus,
you walked on the waters to meet your apostles.
    We pray to you:
Guide the ship of our life
to the shores of eternity.
Save us, O Lord, in the name of your love!

John 2:1-11; 4:46-53; 5:1-8; 6:1-15, 16-21; 9:1-40; 11:1-44.

Lord Jesus,
at Siloam's pool you gave sight to a man born blind.
    We pray to you:
Let your light shine on our world,
pull us out of the darkness of sadness and sin.
Save us, O Lord, in the name of your love!

Lord Jesus,
you called back to life your friend Lazarus
after he had been in his grave four days.
    We pray to you:
On the last day, call us too by our names
and open the door to each grave
that we may, with you and the Holy Spirit,
glorify your Father in eternal joy.
Save us, O Lord, in the name of your love!

THE "OUR FATHER"

According to the Gospel of Luke

One day Jesus was at prayer.
When he had finished,
one of his disciples asked him:
"Lord, teach us to pray
just as John the Baptist taught his disciples."

Jesus said to them:
"Father, hallowed be your name."
    —Your Kingdom come, O Lord!

"Give us each day our daily bread."
    —Your Kingdom come, O Lord!

"Forgive us our sins,
as we ourselves forgive each one
who is in debt to us."
    —Your Kingdom come, O Lord!

"And lead us not into temptation."
    —Your Kingdom come, O Lord!

The "Our Father," *Luke 11:1-4.*

WE ARE THE LEAST OF ALL THE NATIONS

Prayer of the Diaspora

Have mercy, O Lord,
have mercy on us!

Blessed are you, O Lord, God of our fathers,
and glorious forever is your holy name!
But do not forget to have pity on your people!

We have sinned by deserting you,
but do not abandon us,
for the sake of Abraham, your friend,
of Isaac, your servant, and Israel, the holy one.

You promised to multiply your people
like the stars of heaven,
like the grains of sand on the shore of the sea.

But now, we are the least of all the nations,
we are despised throughout the whole world,
humiliated because of our sins.

Accept the sacrifice of our contrite hearts,
let it come into your presence today,
treat us gently as you are gentle and merciful.

We will follow you and seek your face.
Deliver us, Lord, by the power of your love
and give glory to your name,
        through Jesus Christ, your Son,
        our Savior and our brother.

Daniel 3:26-43. *Diaspora* is a Greek word (in Hebrew: *gola*) meaning "dispersion" and designating, in the past, the Jews dispersed outside Palestine, and today the Christian people dispersed all over the world.

WITH THE CHURCH

With the Church in heaven and on earth,
let us glorify the Lord:

Praise to you now and evermore!

With the Virgin Mary, your Mother,
we wish to listen to your Word.
With the patriarchs and prophets,
we wish to announce your Kingdom.

With the apostles and evangelists,
we wish to proclaim the Good News.
With all the disciples who answered your call,
we wish to follow you.

With all the martyrs who offered you their bodies
    in sacrifice,
we wish to give witness to you.
With the saints of all times,
we wish to serve you.

With all those who believe in you,
we offer you the obedience of our faith.
With all those who love you,
we offer you our love.

With all those who seek you in the night,
we wish to walk toward the light.
With all those who are unaware of your name,
we wish to learn to love you.

With all those whom you invite to the banquet
    of the Kingdom,
invite us also, we beg you.
With all those whom you inscribe in the book of life,
count us among your elect.

With all those who die in you,
we place our hope in your mercy.
With all those who have risen with you,
we sing your praises forever.

KING OF ENDLESS GLORY

Praise to you, Lord Jesus Christ, King of endless glory!

> Lord Jesus,
> Bright Morning Star,
> you announce the eternal day —
> we acclaim you!

> Lord Jesus,
> Rising Sun, Light of the World,
> you shine on those in the shadow of death —
> we acclaim you!

> Lord Jesus,
> Living Way to the Father,
> your footprints lead our path to heaven —
> we acclaim you!

> Lord Jesus,
> Living Bread from Heaven,
> come to satisfy the hunger of the world —
> we acclaim you!

> Lord Jesus,
> you who are the Good Shepherd,
> gather all people into one fold —
> we acclaim you!

> Lord Jesus,
> Faithful Witness revealing the Father to us,
> give strength to the testimony
> of those who announce your Word —
> we acclaim you!

> Lord Jesus,
> True Vine of which we are the branches,
> help us to bear much fruit —
> we acclaim you!

> Lord Jesus,
> Firstborn from the dead,
> awaken us when our eternal Day dawns —
> we acclaim you!

Luke 1:78 John 6:32-58; 10:1-16; 14:6; 15:1-17 Colossians 1:15
Revelation 1:5; 22:16.

MAY THEY GLORIFY YOU FOR US, O LORD

Praise to you, Lord Jesus Christ, King of endless glory!

May they glorify you for us, O Lord:
the Virgin Mary who bore you,
the crib wherein you lay as an infant,
the angels who sang in the night to you,
the shepherds who came to adore you.

May they glorify you for us, O Lord:
the Magi who came from the East to you,
the star that shone in your sky,
the little children of Bethlehem
who died for you.

May they glorify you for us, O Lord:
the Jordan that flowed with gladness for you,
the precursor John who baptized you,
the apostles and the disciples
who followed your call.

May they glorify you for us, O Lord:
the children who sang "Hosanna" to you,
the tears of your agony,
the chains that bound you,
the thorns that bruised your forehead.

May they glorify you for us, O Lord:
the Calvary whereon your cross was planted,
the bitter death that you suffered,
the new tomb wherein you rested
in the sleep of death.

May they glorify you for us, O Lord:
the morning which saw your awakening,
the angel in white who announced your resurrection,
the holy women who came to embalm you
and met the angels.

May they glorify you for us, O Lord:
the pain and the joy of all people,
the light of our faith,
the strength of our hope,
the peace that comes from your love.

YOU HAVE COME, LORD

Save us, O Lord,
in the name of your love.

You have come, Lord,
to seek out and save what was lost:
Without you, Lord, we are lost.
    Come to save us!

You have come, Lord,
not to call the just, but sinners:
Without you, Lord, we are crushed by our faults.
    Come to save us!

You have come, Lord,
not to abolish the law, but to fulfill it:
Without you, Lord, we cannot live in love.
    Come to save us!

You have come, Lord,
not to be served, but to serve,
and to give your life as a ransom for many:
Without you, Lord, we cannot serve in truth
    our brothers and sisters.
    Come to save us!

You have come, Lord,
to bring fire upon the earth:
Without you, Lord, we die of cold.
Let the fire of your Spirit burn in us!
    Come to save us!

Matthew 5:17; 9:13   Mark 10:45   Luke 12:49; 19:10. This prayer is based on the
sentence "I came" (from God) or "The Son of Man came." The primitive Christian
community saw in Jesus him "who comes in the name of the Lord"   *(Ps 118:26 =*
Mt 21:9).

GOD OF TENDERNESS

God of tenderness and pity,
slow to anger and full of love,
we pray to you:
    Deliver us, O Lord.

From all sin and every evil,
from the hardening of our hearts,
from all bad will,
    deliver us, O Lord.

From contempt for your Word,
from refusal of your grace,
from the denial of your call,
    deliver us, O Lord.

From the spirit of jealousy and envy,
from pride and vanity,
from indifference toward our brothers and sisters,
    deliver us, O Lord.

From lukewarmness in your love,
from boredom in your service,
from the sadness of this world,
    deliver us, O Lord.

DELIVER US, LORD

Deliver us, O Lord!

By your coming into the world,
by your birth in Bethlehem,
by your hidden life in Nazareth,
    deliver us, O Lord!

By your baptism in the Jordan,
by your fast in the desert,
by your victory over the devil,
    deliver us, O Lord!

By your preaching of the Kingdom,
by your announcement of the Good News,
by your glorious transfiguration,
    deliver us, O Lord!

By your love for the poor,
by your compassion for their sufferings,
by your tears at the tomb of Lazarus,
    deliver us, O Lord!

By your gift of the Eucharist,
by your agony in the garden of Olives,
by your condemnation before Annas and Caiaphas,
    deliver us, O Lord!

By your carrying of the cross,
by your crucifixion and your agony,
by your death and burial,
    deliver us, O Lord!

By your holy resurrection,
by your glorious ascension,
by the coming of the Holy Spirit,
    deliver us, O Lord!

On the day of judgment
may your mercy be our defense;
your love, our salvation.
    Deliver us, O Lord!

WE BEG YOU, LORD

Save us, O Lord,
without you we are lost!

We beg you, Lord!
See our mistakes: be our truth.
See our straying: be our road.
See our death: be our life.
    Save us, O Lord,
without you we are lost!

See our weakness: be our strength.
See our foolishness: be our wisdom.
See our sin: be our pardon.
    Save us, O Lord,
without you we are lost!

See our anguish: be our peace.
See our hunger: be our bread.
See our thirst: be our faith.
    Save us, O Lord,
without you we are lost!

See our pride: be our humility.
See our darkness: be our light.
See our night: be our star.
    Save us, O Lord,
without you we are lost!

Lord Jesus,
you whose name means "Savior,"
    we beg you:
For each of us may your name be true.
Save us all, for you are our brother
    and our only hope!

PRAYER FOR PEOPLE OF ALL AGES

Have mercy, O Lord,
have mercy on us!

Let us pray for all children:
    Help them to grow in grace and wisdom,
    and in the knowledge of your Son Jesus Christ.

Let us pray for all young men and women:
    Give them a full and happy youth;
    open their hearts to accept
    not only the suffering but also the joy of the world.

Let us pray for all married people
        who have promised before Christ to be faithful
            to each other:
    May the fervor of their love show to the world
    the tenderness of Christ Jesus toward his Church.

Let us pray for all those who are single
        because of the Kingdom of heaven:
    Support them in the joy of their vocation,
        that their lives may show to the world the Kingdom
            that is to come.

Let us pray for all those in the autumn of life:
    Grant them a peaceful and happy old age;
    guide their steps on the road to peace.

Let us pray for all those who have no family and home:
    Show the gentleness of your presence
    to all who live alone
    and have no hope but you.

YOU WERE MOVED TO PITY

Lord, have mercy.

You were moved to pity, Lord,
at the sight of the leper who pleaded with you:
"If you wish, you can cure me."
Heal our brothers and sisters who suffer in their flesh,
and cleanse us all of the leprosy of sin,
    we beg you.
Lord, have mercy.

You were moved to pity, Lord,
at the sight of the crowds weary and abandoned
like sheep without a shepherd.
To those in the prison of fatigue or loneliness,
send someone who will guide them toward hope,
    we beg you.
Lord, have mercy.

You were moved to pity, Lord,
at the sight of the crowds who had nothing to eat.
Give each person the bread of earth
and make each one desire the bread of heaven,
    we beg you.
Lord, have mercy.

You were moved to pity, Lord,
at the sight of two blind men by the roadside
who were crying, "Have pity on us, Son of David!"
Be the light of those who are blind,
and heal the blindness of our hearts,
    we beg you.
Lord, have mercy.

You were moved to pity, Lord,
and your heart beat more quickly
when you saw the tears of the widow of Naim.
To those who are sad today,
repeat the words of old, "Do not cry,"
and heal the sadness of our hearts,
    we beg you.
Lord, have mercy.

Mark 1:41; 6:34; 8:2   Matthew 20:34   Luke 7:13   John 11:35.

You were moved to pity, Lord,
when you saw the tears of Martha and Mary.
You yourself wept at your friend's tomb!
Because you are our life and our resurrection,
open a door of hope to each of our troubles,
        we beg you.
Lord, have mercy.

Lord Jesus,
no sorrow is a stranger to you
and all suffering finds the road to your heart.

Consider the misery of all people:
let not their sufferings be in vain;
let them be joined to the merits of your passion
        and to your resurrection.

SONG OF JUBILATION

Blest are you, O Lord, through eternity!

You have hidden your mystery from the wise and the learned.
        Blest are you, O Lord,
        through eternity!

You have revealed it to mere children.
        Blest are you, O Lord,
        through eternity!

Yes, Father, you have graciously willed it so.
        Blest are you, O Lord,
        through eternity!

The prayer "You Were Moved to Pity" is based on *esplagchnisthe,* a verb used by
the Gospels. Literally it means "He was moved by pity in his bowels" — in his
heart, as we would say today.
Song of Jubilation, *Matthew 11:25-27 Luke 10:21-22.*

YOU WERE BORN FOR US IN TIME

Jesus Christ, risen Lord,
have mercy on us!

You were born for us in time,
so you give us eternal life.
You became poor,
so you make us rich.
You became man,
so we become like God.
 We pray to you:
Jesus Christ, risen Lord, have mercy on us!

You received baptism,
so you wash away our sins.
You fasted in the desert,
so you nourish us.
You were tempted by the devil,
so you give us the victory.
 We pray to you:
Jesus Christ, risen Lord, have mercy on us!

You cured the lepers,
so you purify us.
You gave sight to the blind,
so you enlighten us.
You gave speech to the mute,
so you open our mouths to praise.
 We pray to you:
Jesus Christ, risen Lord, have mercy on us!

You were a prisoner,
so you free us.
You kept silent,
so you instruct us.
You were beaten like a slave,
so you set us free.
 We pray to you:
Jesus Christ, risen Lord, have mercy on us!

You were stripped of your clothes,
so you clothe us with glory.
You were given vinegar to drink,
so you quench our thirst.

You were crowned with thorns,
so you make us kings.
    We pray to you:
Jesus Christ, risen Lord, have mercy on us!

You died on the cross,
so you give us life.
You were humiliated unto death,
so you raise us up to heaven.
You were laid in a tomb,
so you raise us to glory.
    We pray to you:
Jesus Christ, risen Lord, have mercy on us!

Help us, Lord,
to serve you with joy,
to glorify you with humility,
to please you with holiness,
to wait for you with hope,
to love you in the peace of the Holy Spirit.
    We pray to you:
Jesus Christ, risen Lord, have mercy on us!

Gather us into your Kingdom,
where you will fill us with joy,
where you will transform all pain,
where you will wipe away every tear,
on that Day when you will create for eternity
the new heavens and the new earth.
    We pray to you:
Jesus Christ, risen Lord, have mercy on us!

According to the Maronite liturgy.

NO ONE IS A FATHER LIKE YOU, LORD

No one is a father
like you, Lord —
you are a father to us!
May you be blest!

Blest are you, O Lord,
through eternity!

You free us from the land of slavery;
you lead us to the kingdom of freedom.
Blest are you, O Lord, through eternity!

As one does for a little child,
you teach us to walk
and hold us in your arms.
Blest are you, O Lord, through eternity!

You lead us with a bridle of kindness;
you guide us with the reins of love.
Blest are you, O Lord, through eternity!

You are like a father to us
who lifts his child to press him close to his cheek,
and you stoop down to us
and give us food.
Blest are you, O Lord, through eternity!

We beg you, Lord:
Because you are our Father,
make us live as your children
so that our entire lives will give you glory,
through Jesus, your Son and our brother.

Hosea 11:1-4.

GLORY TO YOU, FATHER

Glory to you, Father,
through your beloved Son, Jesus Christ,
in the unity of the Holy Spirit!

Blest are you, Lord,
through eternity!

May you be blessed, Father,
because you have created me,
and because the heart that you have given me
you held, first of all, in your own hands!
Blest are you, Lord, through eternity!

May you be blessed, Father,
for the soul that you have given me,
because your love has fashioned it
in the image of Jesus, your firstborn Son!
Blest are you, Lord, through eternity!

May you be blessed, Father,
for the body that you have given me,
because you will call it to live eternally
in the glory of your resurrection!
Blest are you, Lord, through eternity!

O Father of Jesus and source of the Spirit,
you who loved me in Christ
even before the world was created,
you who are the source of my whole being
and the root of every good thing that grows in me:
Because I was born in your heart,
let my whole life be only a return to you —
to your heart, where I will finally know
      the peace of my heart.

Ephesians 1:3-6.

THE PARABLE OF THE SOWER

Remember us, O Lord,
in your loving care!

Jesus taught his disciples with parables.
He said to them, "Listen!
One day a farmer went out sowing...."

So that your Word in us, Lord,
does not fall on the roadside
and Satan remove it from our hearts,
    we pray to you.

So that your Word in us, Lord,
does not fall on rocky ground
and we be fickle
at our first temptation,
    we pray to you.

So that your Word in us, Lord,
does not fall among thorns
and the cares of life
and the enticement of riches choke it,
    we pray to you.

So that your Word in us, Lord,
falls on rich and fertile soil
and we yield fruit in abundance,
    we pray to you.

    Lord Jesus,
sower of all the good that is in the world,
place in us the seeds of goodness and justice.
Let our land yield a harvest of human love
and sheaves of joy for eternal life.

Matthew 13:1-23 Mark 4:1-20 Luke 8:4-15.

GIVE YOUR BREAD

O Lord, we pray to you.

Give your bread, Lord, to those who are hungry;
give hunger for yourself to those who have bread;
    for you alone, Lord,
    can satisfy our desire:
    O Lord, we pray to you.

Give your strength to those who are weak;
give humility to those who think themselves strong;
    for you alone, Lord,
    are our strength:
    O Lord, we pray to you.

Give faith to those who are in doubt;
give doubt to those who believe they possess you;
    for you alone, Lord,
    are the truth:
    O Lord, we pray to you.

Give confidence to those who are afraid;
give your fear to those who have too much confidence;
    for you alone, Lord,
    support our hope:
    O Lord, we pray to you.

Give light to those who are searching for you;
preserve in your love those who have found you;
    for you alone, Lord,
    can fulfill our love:
    O Lord, we pray to you.

COME TO ME LIKE A CRY OF JOY

Come, Lord Jesus Christ!

When my life sinks in sadness,
come to me like a cry of joy.
    Come, Lord Jesus Christ!

When my heart is as hard as a rock,
come to me like the dew of springtime.
    Come, Lord Jesus Christ!

When noise invades my haven,
come to me like an oasis of silence.
    Come, Lord Jesus Christ!

When the wind of hate rises within me,
come to me like a kiss of pardon.
    Come, Lord Jesus Christ!

When I am sinking into the darkness of death,
come to me like a child's smile.
    Come, Lord Jesus Christ!

And when the earth encloses me in its arms,
open for me the doors of your mercy.
    Come, Lord Jesus Christ!

YOU HAVE LOVED OUR EARTH, LORD JESUS

May you be blest, O Lord!

You have loved our earth, Lord Jesus,
in the many-colored flowers of the fields
more beautiful than the robe of Solomon,
and in the birds of the sky who worship the Father
by their flapping wings and their joyous chirping —
you said they are the sign of his providence!
    May you be blest, O Lord!

You have loved our earth, Lord,
as you admired the wedding dress of the bride.
It is beautiful, you said, like the grace
we must have to enter the banquet of the Kingdom.
    May you be blest, O Lord!

You have loved our earth, Lord,
in the street children playing their pipes and dancing,
and in the little ones brought to you in their mothers' arms.
You loved and even embraced them!
    May you be blest, O Lord!

You have loved our earth, Lord,
in the sweet-smelling perfume, which fills the house,
and in Mary's hair drying your feet.
You defended her!
    May you be blest, O Lord!

You have loved our earth, Lord,
in the lightning flash of the storm,
splitting the sky from the east to the west.
Its suddenness, you said, is a sign of the coming Kingdom
that will burst upon the world.
    May you be blest, O Lord!

You have loved the crimson sky in the evening —
it is the throne of God, you said.
It transfigures the earth,
which you called God's footstool!
    May you be blest, O Lord!

Matthew 5:35; 6:28-30; 22:11-12; 24:27 Luke 7:31-32; 17:23-24 John 12:3-8.

You have loved our earth, Lord:
When you saw a bird's nest,
you dreamed of a place to lay your head —
which you, O Son of Man, had not!
   May you be blest, O Lord!

You have loved our earth, Lord:
You watched the budding wheat,
hurrying to grow day and night,
so as to ripen as surely as your Kingdom comes.
   May you be blest, O Lord!

You have loved our earth, Lord:
You allowed yourself to be caressed by the evening breeze,
which wanders through the byways of Jerusalem,
as mysterious as the passing of your Spirit.
   May you be blest, O Lord!

You have loved our earth, Lord:
When you foresaw the morning star
gleaming through the rosy light of dawn,
you thought of your own mystery —
you who are for all who seek you
the shining star of eternal morning!
   May you be blest, O Lord!

We beg you, Lord:
Because you have loved our earth,
which has become yours by your birth in Bethlehem,
make us, too, by loving it,
learn to prefer heaven to it
until the day when you will create for eternity
the new heavens and the new earth.

Matthew 8:20 Mark 4:26-29 John 3:8 Revelation 22:16.

YOU CHOOSE THE WEAK

The powerful of the world are held in esteem,
but it is the weak whom you have chosen.
  We bless you:
Blest are you, O Lord, through eternity!

The learned people of the world are proud,
but it is the simple whom you embrace.
  We bless you:
Blest are you, O Lord, through eternity!

Those who claim a noble birth are proud,
but it is those who are despised, those with no name,
whom you have chosen as your brothers and sisters.
  We bless you:
Blest are you, O Lord, through eternity!

The wisdom of the world is tempting,
but it is the folly of the cross that you prefer.
  We bless you:
Blest are you, O Lord, through eternity!

  Lord Jesus,
you who save us through your cross of light,
which is a scandal and a folly for pagans,
but a power of salvation for those who believe,
  we implore you:
Give us that supreme wisdom
to accept our weakness,
so as to be saved only by the power of your love,
you who are the God of the humble
and the friend of the poor.

1 Corinthians 1:18-31.

PRAYER OF THE BEATITUDES

Blest are those who are invited to the banquet of the Kingdom.

Lord Jesus, you said,
"Blest are the poor in spirit;
the reign of God is theirs."
Give us the spirit of poverty and humility.

Lord Jesus, you said,
"Blest too are the sorrowing;
they shall be consoled."
Teach us to share the tears of our brothers and sisters.

Lord Jesus, you said,
"Blest are the lowly;
they shall inherit the land."
Give us a heart as lowly and humble as yours.

Lord Jesus, you said,
"Blest are they who hunger and thirst for holiness;
they shall have their fill."
Give us souls athirst for justice and love.

Lord Jesus, you said,
"Blest are they who show mercy;
mercy shall be theirs."
Open our hearts with love for our brothers and sisters.

Lord Jesus, you said,
"Blest are the single-hearted,
for they shall see God."
Enlighten our eyes with your splendor.

Lord Jesus, you said,
"Blest too are the peacemakers;
they shall be called children of God."
Make us channels of peace and joy.

Lord Jesus, you said,
"Blest are those persecuted for righteousness' sake;
the reign of God is theirs."
Make us strong in suffering for the Kingdom.

Matthew 5:3-12.

MAY IT RISE

*Let the light of your face
shine upon us!*

May the kindness of your face
    rise above the hardness of our hearts.
May the humility of your heart
    rise above the foolishness of our pride.
Let the light of your face shine upon us!

May the joy of your mercy
    rise above the sadness of our sins.
May the splendor of your eternal Day
    rise above the sleep of our death.
Let the light of your face shine upon us!

May the freedom of the children of God
    rise above our slavery.
May the peace of your love
    rise above our anguish.
Let the light of your face shine upon us!

May the dawn of your resurrection
    rise above the night of our world.
May the glory of God
    rise within the heart of each person.
Let the light of your face shine upon us!

"I AM"

Remember us, O Lord,
in your Kingdom.

Lord Jesus, you said,
"I am the bread of life."
Satisfy our hunger for eternity,
    we pray to you.

Lord Jesus, you said,
"I am the light of the world."
Light up our darkness with your splendor,
    we pray to you.

Lord Jesus, you said,
"I am the gate of the sheepfold."
Lead us to your Kingdom,
    we pray to you.

Lord Jesus, you said,
"I am the good shepherd."
Gather us into your fold,
    we pray to you.

Lord Jesus, you said,
"I am the resurrection and the life."
Awaken us from the sleep of death,
    we pray to you.

Lord Jesus, you said,
"I am the way, the truth, and the life."
Show us the face of your Father,
    we pray to you.

Lord Jesus, you said,
"I am the true vine."
Help us to bear fruit in your love,
    we pray to you.

John 6:35; 8:12; 10:7; 11:25; 14:6; 15:1. The prayer "I Am" is based on the *Ego eimi* sentences of the Gospel of John. Jesus affirms that he is for the messianic people what Yahve ("I am who am." *Exodus 3:14*) was for the people of the Exodus.

GOD OF OUR CHILDHOOD

Remember us, O Lord,
in your loving care.

God of our childhood,
you whose name we have learned
in the smiles of our father and mother,
    we beg you:
Preserve in us a childlike spirit
so that we can enter your Kingdom.

God of our adolescence,
you who have created the eagerness of youth,
who know its desires and its follies,
    we beg you:
Preserve the flower of hope in our hearts;
be always the God of the joy of our youth.

God of our maturity,
you who call us
to make fruitful the gifts you have put in us,
    we beg you:
Help each of us to become that perfect Man
who realizes the fullness of Christ.

God of our old age,
at the time when the spirit loses its ardor,
when the body becomes feeble,
    we beg you:
Remain close to us when the night comes.
You are our God for all eternity.

Ephesians 4:13.

HOLY ARE YOUR WAYS!

Holy, holy, holy is the Lord,
for eternal is his love!

It is written in the psalm:
"O God, holy are your ways!"

Holy is the journey of my life toward you
and the way from my captivity to your freedom.
> Holy, holy is the Lord,
> for eternal is his love!

Holy is the joy that stirs me with enthusiasm
and makes me run swiftly on your road.
> Holy, holy is the Lord,
> for eternal is his love!

Holy are the troubles that crush me with weariness
and that slow down my progress.
> Holy, holy is the Lord,
> for eternal is his love!

Holy are the meetings with all my friends
who journey with me toward your dwelling.
> Holy, holy is the Lord,
> for eternal is his love!

Holy, too, is the death that awaits me at the road's end,
for then I will be very close to your home!
> Holy, holy is the Lord,
> for eternal is his love!

Help me to understand, Lord,
that what counts is not the road traveled,
but simply putting my hand in yours
and journeying side by side with you, Lord Jesus —
O you who are the joy of my journey
and also the repose in the Father's home!
> Holy, holy is the Lord,
> for eternal is his love!

Psalm 77:14 Hebrews 13:14.

WATCH OVER YOUR CHURCH

O Lord, we pray to you.

Watch over your Church;
    make it perfect in your love.
O Lord, we pray to you.

Gather all the baptized
    into the unity of the faith.
O Lord, we pray to you.

Lead all people
    to the light of the Gospel.
O Lord, we pray to you.

Give to all people
    peace with justice.
O Lord, we pray to you.

To those who remember the poor
    give everlasting reward.
O Lord, we pray to you.

Strengthen all our brothers and sisters
    in the service of the Kingdom.
O Lord, we pray to you.

Lift our souls
    toward the desires of heaven.
O Lord, we pray to you.

Give to our deceased brothers and sisters
    life in eternal light.
O Lord, we pray to you.

AN ANGEL SPOKE THROUGH MY DARKNESS

Open my eyes, O Jesus, Lord!

An angel spoke through my darkness:
"Clothe your soul with light
and you will find the day,
    Christ Jesus."
Open my eyes, O Jesus, Lord!

An angel spoke through my pain:
"Clothe your soul with patience
and you will find peace,
    Christ Jesus."
Open my eyes, O Jesus, Lord!

An angel spoke through my agony:
"Clothe your soul with confidence
and you will find rest,
    Christ Jesus."
Open my eyes, O Jesus, Lord!

An angel spoke through my dying:
"Clothe your soul in life
and you will find eternity,
    Christ Jesus."
Open my eyes, O Jesus, Lord!

LIFE OF MY LIFE

My Lord and my God!

Life of my life,
keep my heart pure
and make your dwelling there!
    My Lord and my God!

Light of my light,
disperse my darkness
so that I can see you!
    My Lord and my God!

Truth beyond truth,
drive falsehood from me
so that my life will be transparent.
    My Lord and my God!

Joy of my joy,
preserve me from sadness
so that your smile will blossom on my lips.
    My Lord and my God!

And when evening comes,
let the dawn of eternal life
rise for me!
    My Lord and my God!

JESUS, WORD OF THE FATHER

Praise to you, O Lord!
or *Save us, O Lord, in the name of your love!*

Jesus, Word of the Father,	*Jn 1:1*
Jesus, everlasting Wisdom,	*1 Cor 1:24*
Jesus, Son of God.	*Rom 1:4*
Jesus, Son of Man,	
Jesus, Son of David,	
Jesus, Son of Abraham.	*Mt 1:1*
Jesus, Son of Mary,	
Jesus, Son of Joseph,	*Mt 1:16*
Jesus, the Carpenter.	*Mk 6:3*
Jesus, the Messiah,	*Jn 1:41; 4:25*
Jesus, the Emmanuel,	*Mt 1:23*
Jesus, "the One who comes	
in the name of the Lord."	*Mk 11:9; Lk 13:35*
Jesus, the light of the world,	*Jn 8:12*
Jesus, sun of justice,	*Mal 4:2*
Jesus, morning star.	*Rv 22:16*
Jesus, living path to the Father,	*Heb 10:19*
Jesus, our life,	
Jesus, our truth.	*Jn 14:6*
Jesus, the Holy and Just,	*Acts 13:14*
Jesus, the Advocate,	*1 Jn 2:1*
Jesus, the just Judge.	*2 Tm 4:6-8*
Jesus, the new Adam,	*1 Cor 15:45*
Jesus, our life,	*Jn 1:4*
Jesus, our resurrection.	*Jn 11:25*
Jesus, priest of the New Covenant,	*Heb 8:6*
Jesus, merciful and faithful priest,	*Heb 2:17*
Jesus, mediator between God and man.	*1 Tm 2:5*
Jesus, the good shepherd,	*Jn 10:11*
Jesus, gate of the sheepfold,	*Jn 10:7*
Jesus, Lamb of God.	*Jn 1:29*

Jesus, prophet risen from among us,	*Lk 7:16*
Jesus, our Master,	*Mk 9:5*
Jesus, meek and humble of heart.	*Mt 11:29*
Jesus, our peace,	*Eph 2:14*
Jesus, our Redeemer,	*1 Cor 1:30*
Jesus, ransom for our sins.	*1 Jn 4:10; Mk 10:45*
Jesus, the Savior,	*Mt 1:21*
Jesus, Prince of life,	*Acts 3:15*
Jesus, Head of our faith.	*Heb 12:2*
Jesus, light of life,	*Jn 8:12*
Jesus, bread of heaven,	*Jn 6:35*
Jesus, living water springing to eternal life.	*Jn 4:10*
Jesus, our justice,	
Jesus, our holiness,	
Jesus, our redemption.	*1 Cor 1:30*
Jesus, beloved Son,	*Eph 1:6*
Jesus, firstborn of many brothers and sisters,	*Rom 8:29*
Jesus, our Amen to the glory of the Father.	*2 Cor 2:19*
Jesus, cornerstone of the Church,	*Acts 4:11*
Jesus, rock of Israel,	*1 Cor 10:4*
Jesus, spouse of the messianic community.	*2 Cor 11:2*
Jesus, resurrected Lord,	*Rom 10:9*
Jesus, Savior of the world,	*1 Jn 4:14; Jn 4:42*
Jesus, king of justice and peace.	*Mt 21:5; Heb 7:2*
Jesus, Wonderful Counselor,	
Jesus, Divine Hero,	
Jesus, Prince of peace.	*Is 9:6*
Jesus, faithful Witness,	*Rv 1:5*
Jesus, Firstborn from among the dead,	*Col 1:18*
Jesus, Prince of the kings of the earth.	*Rv 1:5*
Jesus, Image of the invisible God,	*Col 1:15*
Jesus, Splendor of his glory,	*Heb 1:3*
Jesus, Son and Heir.	*Heb 1:2*

Jesus, true Vine of which we are the branches,	*Jn 15:1*
Jesus, Firstborn of all creatures,	*Col 1:15*
Jesus, Head of the Body, your Church.	*Col 1:18*

Jesus, the First and the Last, the Living One,	*Rv 1:17*
Jesus, the Alpha and the Omega,	*Rv 1:8; 21:6*
Jesus, the Beginning and the End.	*Rv 22:13*

JESUS, THE NEW COVENANT

You are my love, O Lord,
you are my joy!

Jesus, the New Covenant,
Jesus, our peace,
pardon for our sins.

Jesus, the Holy and Just One,
Jesus, the Messiah,
Jesus, the Emmanuel.

Jesus, the road to the Father,
Jesus, our life
and our truth.

Jesus, light of the world,
Sun of justice,
Morning Star.

Jesus, meek and humble Messiah,
Shepherd of Israel,
and gate of the sheepfold.

Jesus, eternal Word,
and the Word made flesh,
Wisdom of the Most High.

Jesus, Son of Mary,
Jesus, the Savior,
Jesus, Son of God.

SONG OF CREATION

Blest are you, O Lord,
through eternity!

For you, O Lord of eternity,
    creation celebrates;
of the brightness of your infinite splendor
    its beauty sings.
For you the birds
    lift their voices in the trees;
you are he whom their flapping wings
    try to adore.
Blest are you, O Lord, through eternity!

For you the sheep
    romp in the fields
and the lambs dance on their feet
    among the scarlet poppies.
For you the fish glide in the water;
    before your face they jump for joy.
For you the clouds leap across the heavens,
    and the wind's murmur travels the hills.
Blest are you, O Lord, through eternity!

You are he who hears the chick speak in its shell
    and fills it with the breath of life.
You alone give it strength to break its egg and cry
    so it can call its mother.
You are he who created the rivers in the sky
    and the waves of rain upon the mountains.
Your sun sends its rays to nourish the prairie
    and bleach the desert rocks.
Blest are you, O Lord, through eternity!

You are he who opens the doors
    for the shades of night,
who strokes the horizon
    with the fingers of dawn.
Yours is the sun whose heat leaps up in the east,
    a fountain of life.
You are he who clothes the earth with your beauty,
    yours is the lightning that splits the clouds.
Blest are you, O Lord, through eternity!

You are he who directs the dance of the seasons
    and makes the jonquils bloom in the meadows.
At the kiss of your warmth
    the grain of the wheat in the ground feels comfort.
You are he who clothes the flowers of the field
    with their colorful garb.
Before your face they open their mouths
    to drink their fullness of warmth.
Blest are you, O Lord, through eternity!

You are he who gives unto a man the seed
    to conceive a child
    in the womb of its mother;
you are he who comforts him so he does not cry,
    who opens his mouth,
    and who teaches him speech.
You are he who instills in the heart of a husband
    his love for his wife,
and in a father his laugh when he sees his own self
    in the eyes of his child.
Blest are you, O Lord, through eternity!

Wonderful are your works, O Lord:
    You created the world to show us your love!
You give food to each of us
    and you measure the length of our days.
You send forth your Spirit and all are created,
    and the face of the earth you renew.
You, God, are alone — none other like you!
    All creation takes life from your beauty.
And you live in my heart —
    it is there that I know you!
Blest are you, O Lord, through eternity!

To all who admire your beauty, O Lord,
in the work of your hands,
some day let your face shine forth in its splendor
with the sweetness of your love as Father
    in the face of Jesus your Son,
    the firstborn of all creatures!

This text was inspired (partially) by the sapiential literature of Egypt, particularly by a poem of Akhenaton (fourteenth century before Jesus Christ). That
poem itself inspired *Psalm 104* of the Bible.

WE GIVE YOU THANKS

Prayer of the Didache

We thank you, Father,
for the holy vine of David, your servant,
which you have revealed through Jesus, your Son.
    Praise to you now and evermore!

We thank you, Father,
for the life and the knowledge
that you have revealed through Jesus, your Son.
    Praise to you now and evermore!

Just as this bread that we break
    was once distributed on a hillside
and its fragments gathered so as not to lose any,
so let your Church be gathered
from the farthest parts of the earth into your Kingdom.
    Praise to you now and evermore!

Because yours are the glory and the power forever.
    Praise to you now and evermore!

We thank you, holy Father,
for your holy name that dwells in our hearts.
    Praise to you now and evermore!

For the knowledge, the faith, and the immortality
that you have revealed to us through Jesus, your Son.
    Praise to you now and evermore!

It is you, all-powerful Master, who created the universe
    in praise of your name.
    Praise to you now and evermore!

You give food and drink to the children of men;
but to us you give the grace of a spiritual food,
of a drink for eternal life through Jesus, your Son.
    Praise to you now and evermore!

Above all, we thank you for your power.
    Praise to you now and evermore!

Remember, Lord, your Church,
to deliver it from every evil,
and to make it perfect in your love.
Praise to you now and evermore!

Gather together from the four winds
this santified Church
into the kingdom that you have prepared.
Praise to you now and evermore!

Come, Lord, and let this world pass!   —*Amen.*
Hosanna to the house of David!   —*Amen.*
Let him who is holy come!   —*Amen.*
Let him who is not, repent!   —*Amen.*
Marana tha (Come, Lord)!   —*Amen.*

THE GREAT PRAYER
of
Clement of Rome

Praise to you, O Lord!

May the Creator of the universe
keep intact the number of his elect in the whole world,
 through Jesus Christ, your beloved Son.
 Praise to you, O Lord!

Through him you have called us from the darkness
 into the light,
from ignorance to the full knowledge of your glory,
to the hope of your name, source of all creation.
 Praise to you, O Lord!

You have opened the eyes of our hearts
 so that they recognize you,
you, the only Most High in the highest heavens,
the Holy One who dwells among the saints.
 Praise to you, O Lord!

You humble the insolence of the proud;
you defeat the plans of nations;
you exalt the humble; you humble the powerful.
 Praise to you, O Lord!

You enrich and you make poor;
you give death; you save and give life,
unique Benefactor of spirits and the God of all creation.
 Praise to you, O Lord!

You contemplate the abyss;
you survey the works of humans,
you, the help of those who are in danger,
their Savior in despair,
Creator and guardian of every spirit!
 Praise to you, O Lord!

You multiply the peoples of the earth,
and, from among them all, you choose those who love you,
through Jesus Christ, your beloved Son;
through him you have instructed, sanctified, and glorified us.
 Praise to you, O Lord!

We pray to you, O Master,
that you be our help and our support.
Lord, listen to us!

The afflicted — save them;
the lowly — have pity on them.
Lord, listen to us!

The fallen — lift them up;
the needy — give yourself to them.
Lord, listen to us!

The sick — cure them;
your people who have strayed — bring them home.
Lord, listen to us!

Fill those who are hungry;
free those who are prisoners.
Lord, listen to us!

Strengthen those who are feeble;
console those who are fearful.
Lord, listen to us!

May all peoples recognize that you alone are God,
that Jesus Christ is your Son,
that we are your people and the sheep of your pasture.
Lord, listen to us!

Clement of Rome, "Letter to the Corinthians" (about 95-96).

LET US CALL UPON GOD WITH FAITH

Let us call with faith upon God our Father,
through Jesus Christ, his beloved Son,
in the Holy Spirit, who inspires our prayer:
    Remember us, O Lord,
    in your loving care!

For the spotless Church of Jesus Christ,
that it may show forth unto the world
    the glory of the Lord,
let us ask for the riches of divine goodness.
Remember us, O Lord, in your loving care!

For those who faithfully dispense
    the word of truth,
for those who exercise authority
    in the service of their brothers and sisters,
let us ask for the infinite wisdom of the Word of God.
Remember us, O Lord, in your loving care!

For those who live in celibacy
    for the sake of the Kingdom of heaven,
for those who labor and spend themselves
    in spiritual works,
let us call upon him who bestows the gifts of the Spirit.
Remember us, O Lord, in your loving care!

For those who direct the people,
that they may govern according to right and justice,
let us call upon the King of kings and Master of nations.
Remember us, O Lord, in your loving care!

For those who are beginning to know
    the name of the Lord Jesus
and ardently desire divine mercy,
let us call upon him who is the way, the truth, and the life.
Remember us, O Lord, in your loving care!

For those held captive
    by human weakness and frailty,
    by the spirit of envy and hatred,
    by the many errors of the world,
let us implore the mercy of our Redeemer.
Remember us, O Lord, in your loving care!

For those who suffer
    in their flesh or their spirit,
those oppressed, slandered, or hopeless,
let us call upon the Lord who is close to despondent hearts.
Remember us, O Lord, in your loving care!

For those who have been victims of error or lies,
those who do not know the light of the Gospel,
    for those who despise it,
let us call upon the Lord of truth.
Remember us, O Lord, in your loving care!

For those whose love comes to the aid of the poor,
those who share their bread
    with their less fortunate brothers and sisters,
let us pray to the Lord, the friend of the poor.
Remember us, O Lord, in your loving care!

For all of us gathered here,
that we may receive our daily bread
    and pardon for our sins,
let us call upon our Father in heaven.
Remember us, O Lord, in your loving care!

For our brothers and sisters who have left this world,
that they enjoy eternal light and peace,
let us pray to Jesus Christ, firstborn from the dead.
Remember us, O Lord, in your loving care!

Based on the prayer which Pope Gelasius (492-496) "prescribed for singing by
the universal Church."

THE FIRSTBORN OF MANY

Lord Jesus,
you came among us,
the firstborn of many brothers and sisters.

You have walked upon our earth;
you have eaten our bread;
your eyes have seen our light;
your smile has lit up our faces;
and our tears have dampened your eyes.
    We pray to you:

Because you became like us
in all things except sin,
make us like you in grace.

Send us your Holy Spirit
that he may fashion us for eternity.
May your Father recognize your voice in our prayer.
May he say to each one of us:
"This is my Son, my beloved.
My favor rests on him!"

Listen to us, Lord:
We are your Church;
we are your Body, and flesh of your flesh.
You are our God and our brother,
forever and ever.
    Amen!

Matthew 3:17 Romans 8:29 Hebrews 4:15.

TO SAVE US

God our Father,
who send your Son Jesus Christ into the world
not to judge it but to save it,
  listen to our prayer:

By giving us your Son, you offer each of us
your light for our darkness,
your joy for our sadness,
your bread to nourish our life,
and your life to overcome our death.

Open our hearts to your word and your grace
so that we may recognize
in you, our Father who calls us by our name,
in your Son, our Savior and brother,
in your Spirit, the love that unites us.

And while our lips sing your praise,
bring our hearts close to you,
through Jesus Christ, our Lord.
  Amen.

John 12:47.

SOURCE OF ALL JOY

God our Father, source of all joy,
    we pray to you:

Help us to understand
that our heaven begins today
when we seek and learn to love you
in the service of our brothers and sisters.

Reveal also your Church to all people.
Let it be the land of their liberty;
let their faces shine
    with the joy of your Son.

FIRE ON THE EARTH

For a long time I have given up
trying to revive the ashes of my dreams.
My hearth is dead.

But you, Lord — did you not come
to bring fire on the earth?

Burn my heart
with the flame of your heart,
you who alone can change
the ashes of my dreams
into a fire of love.

Luke 12:49.

YOUR LOVE FILLS THE EARTH

God our Father, you who tell us
that your love fills the earth
and that your tenderness is for each person
that of a father for his children,
    we pray to you:

Make your light shine in our hearts
so that we can recognize
that your Word is true,
and that your love rests upon each of us
when you give us your only Son, Jesus Christ.

Give us the grace, Lord,
to look for you in the love of our brothers and sisters,
to discover your name in their faces,
to meet you in the heart of our life,
and to reveal to all people
that you wish to fill them with your joy and peace,

in Christ Jesus, your Son,
our Savior and our brother.
    Amen.

Psalm 33:5; 103:13.

"I DESPISE YOUR FEASTS"

Lord God,
by the mouth of your prophet Amos you tell us:
"I hate and despise your feasts;
I want none of your holocausts.
Let me have no more of the din of your chanting,
no more of your strumming on harps.
But let justice flow like water,
and righteousness like an unfailing stream."

Because you judge us by our hearts
and not by our songs,
because you judge us by the depth of our love
and not by the weight of our offerings,
     we beg you:

Let our feast be to come to the aid
     of the poor and the oppressed,
our song be to practice justice,
and our holocaust be the offering
     of a contrite and humble heart.

Then, when our lips sing to you,
our hearts will be celebrating a feast
and you will love our song.

Amos 5:21-24.

PRAYER OF THE LONELY

Lord, listen to me.
Even surrounded by my friends,
I sometimes feel loneliness that enters my heart
like the sorrow of a winter night.

So I beg you:
Give me as my family
all the angels and the saints
who live in your presence.
Let them speak to me about you,
those who know how much you love us.

Then, with a happy heart,
I will go to find my brothers and sisters to tell them
that you are expecting all of us in your home
for the eternal celebration.

ONE UPON WHOM YOU CAST YOUR EYES

Heaven is your throne, Lord,
and the earth is your footstool.
Every wonderful thing that we can offer you
for a dwelling
your hand has given us.

But the one upon whom you cast your eyes
is the one who is poor and has a contrite heart,
the one who reveres your word.

Lord, fill our hearts with poverty
so that they may become
a worthy dwelling place for your glory.

Ephesians 2:19 Isaiah 66:1.

LIKE CHILDREN

Like children playing on the beach,
we have built houses of sand.
The wave of time has come
and the laughter of the tides has submerged
    everything.

But we know, Lord,
that, if our earthly home is destroyed,
you will build us an eternal home
    near you in heaven.

Give us the strength to leave our earthly
    dwellings
and our games in the sand.
Direct our boats
toward the shores of eternity.

TO EACH OF US OUR SHARE OF JOY AND HAPPINESS

Lord Jesus,
God of all tenderness
and of all mercy,
you who spent your time on earth doing good,
    we pray to you:
Give to each of us our share of joy and happiness,
so that we can, on our road of life,
discover your love constantly,
bless and glorify you,
and arrive at perfect joy,
which is to live near your Father,
with you and the Holy Spirit,
forever and ever.
    Amen!

2 Corinthians 5:1 Acts 10:38.

USELESS SERVANTS

For your love, Lord, we labor all day long;
for your Kingdom, we struggle all our lives.

And now you tell us:
"You are useless servants."

We are delighted, Lord,
to be such servants.
For we can now implore you:
Give us your Kingdom for nothing,
that is, simply because you love us,
and because Jesus Christ is our brother.

YOU WHO MEASURE THE OCEANS

You, Lord, who measure the oceans in the hollow
    of your hand,
who calculate the dimensions of the heavens
    with your extended fingers,
you who weigh the mountains in scales,
and the hills in a balance,

You before whom the nations
are like a drop of water on the rim of a pail,
like a grain of dust on the scales —
You, the wonderful and magnificent Lord,
    we beg you:

Remember that we are dust
and that from the dust you formed
    the body of your Son Jesus,
our Savior and our brother forever.

Luke 17:10   Isaiah 40:12-15.

MY WORDS WITHER AWAY

Lord of glory and of pity,
my words wither away in singing of your beauty;
my music breaks apart before your grandeur;
and to reecho your love,
I find myself without melody.

Accept my weariness as praise;
take my silence
    as a song of joy.

WONDERFUL IS OUR LIFE

The whole day long the bee has buzzed with joy;
the flower has sung its song with color;
the leaf of the tree has trembled with pleasure.

Your creation is wonderful, Lord!

More wonderful still is our life,
because you fill it with your presence
and your smile pours over our faces
    with your beauty.

PRAYER FOR MISSIONARIES

With the apostle Paul, we pray, Lord,
for all engaged in missionary labor.

May they serve the Lord with complete humility
    in the midst of their trials.
May their own lives seem less important in their sight
than the mission they have received from the Lord Jesus:
to bear witness to the Good News of God's graciousness.

May they never recoil from the necessity
of announcing the entire design of God.
May they carefully watch over the flock
that the Holy Spirit has entrusted to their care.

May they not covet anyone's money.
May the work of their hands provide
for their needs and for those of the poor.

May they remember the words of Jesus:
"There is more happiness in giving
than receiving."

May they, even today, receive
the reward promised to missionaries:
the daily, ever increasing joy
    of laboring for the sake of your Kingdom.

Paul's farewell address to the elders of the Church of Ephesus, *Acts 20:18-35.*

FOR THE AUTHORITIES OF THE CHURCH

We pray, God our Father,
for those who hold authority in the Church:

May they shepherd the flock of God
    that is entrusted to them.
May they watch over it not merely as a duty,
    but gladly, because God wants it;
not for love of sordid gain,
    but with devotion of heart;
not acting as dictators over their brothers and sisters,
    but as examples that the whole flock can follow.

And when Christ, the chief Shepherd, returns,
may they receive the reward promised
    to the sheep that you love.

THE HARVEST IS ABUNDANT

"The harvest is abundant,
but the laborers are few."
    We ask you, Lord:
Send laborers to your harvest!

May they announce the Kingdom
and cure the sick.

As they travel, may they take along
neither the power of money
nor the strength of brute force,
but only your peace.

May their entire lives proclaim:
"The Kingdom of God is very near to you!"

1 Peter 5:1-5 Luke 9:1-5; 10:1-12.

AS A DOE

As a doe longs for running water,
so my soul longs for you, my God!

My soul thirsts for God, the living God:
When shall I go to see your face,
    O Father of Jesus,
    my Christ and my brother,
    and source of the Spirit,
    love in my heart!

MY SOUL THIRSTS FOR YOU

God — it is you, my God — I search for you!
My soul thirsts for you
like a parched, weary, waterless land!

For me, your love, Lord,
is better than life.

I sing for joy in the shadow of your wings;
my soul clings close to you.

Be my help, O my God,
in your Son Jesus Christ.

Psalms 42, 63.

AS A CHILD IN ITS MOTHER'S ARMS

Lord, when I pray,
too often I get so taken up with words
that I no longer hear your voice.

But today I want to keep my soul at peace before you
as a child in its mother's arms.

Let my words become silence,
and let my silence become prayer.

YOU HAVE LAID YOUR HAND ON ME

Lord, you have laid your hand on me;
Lord, you have called me by name.
    I beg you:
Keep me in the palm of your hand;
do not forget my name;
call me to you.

BE PERFECT

Our Father in heaven,
your Son Jesus tells us,
"Be perfect
as your heavenly Father is perfect."

Because he asks the impossible of us,
    we beg you:
Accept, in our place, the offering of
    your beloved Son —
he alone is as perfect as you.

Psalm 131   Psalm 139:5   Matthew 5:48.

A FAMINE OF THE WORD

Thus speaks the Lord:
"See what days are coming
when I will bring famine on the country,
a famine not of bread, a drought not of water,
but of hearing the Word of the Lord."

See, Lord God, our distress:
We have eaten the bitter bread of our illusions
    without being satisfied.
And we have drunk water from our old wells
    without quenching our thirst.

But now we want no more
    than your Word alone,
    your Son Jesus Christ,
    bread of eternal life!

YOUR WORD, LORD

Your Word, Lord — is it not in the heavens?
So we must say:
"Who will go up to heaven for us
and bring it down to us,
so that we may hear it
and keep it?"

Your Word, Lord — is it not beyond the seas?
So we must say:
"Who will cross the seas for us
and bring it back for us,
so that we may hear it
and keep it?"

Your Word, Lord, is very near to us;
it is your Son Jesus Christ,
living in our hearts.

Amos 8:11 Deuteronomy 30:11-14.

LIKE THE PATRIARCH ENOCH

Grant us the same grace, O Lord,
that you gave to the patriarch Enoch.
It is written in the Holy Book:
"Enoch walked with God."

Day after day,
and during every moment of each day,
allow us to place our hands in yours
and walk with you.

LIKE ABRAHAM

Like Abraham,
I have left everything, Lord,
and no longer have a dwelling place.

Now, Lord, give me your mercy
for a dwelling place.

FOR I AM ALONE

Prayer of Esther

O my Lord, our God, no one is like you!
Come to my aid, for I am alone;
I have no recourse but you.
Listen to the voice of the hopeless!
Deliver us from evil;
free us from all anguish.

Save us
through your Son Jesus Christ.

Genesis 5:24; 12:1-4 Esther 4:17(Vg).

YOU HAVE SEDUCED ME, LORD

You have seduced me, Lord,
and I have let myself be seduced.
You have overpowered me,
for you were the stronger.

Continue, Lord, I beg you,
to hold my heart in your hand.
Let me see in all human love
    a spark of your love,
and in all the beauty of the earth
    the reflection of your splendor.

IN THE POTTER'S HAND

Like clay in the hands of the potter,
so are we in your hands, Lord.

Reveal to us the richness of your glory:
We are vases filled with your mercy.

LIKE THE MORNING MIST

Look, Lord, at our weakness.

Our love for you is like the morning mist
that dissolves at the first ray of sunlight,
like the dew at dawn
that is dried up by the first breath of wind.

Give us, Lord, give us
a love simple and pure,
a love that the heat of evil cannot dry up,
that the breath of doubt cannot touch,
a love simple and pure
like the love of a child for its father.

Jeremiah 20:7; 18:1-12　Romans 9:23　Hosea 6:4.

MAY YOU BE BLESSED, LORD

May you be blessed, Lord, because you are God:
 the help of the oppressed,
 the support of the weak,
 the refuge of the forsaken,
 the savior of the despairing.
May you be blessed, Lord, because you are our God!

GO, EAT YOUR BREAD WITH JOY

 God our Father,
you have said to each of us:
"Go, eat your bread with joy!"
 We pray to you:

Give each of us, along with our daily bread,
our share of joy and happiness,
so that we may recognize you as God
and may love you as Father.

HAPPY THE POOR

 Lord Jesus, you love the poor,
and you declare them "happy,"
for theirs is the Kingdom of heaven.
 We pray:

Give us hearts so poor
that they may be enriched
 by your love.

We ask this of you
in the name of your Son Jesus,
who, though he was rich,
 made himself poor
to enrich us by his poverty.

Judith 9:11 Ecclesiastes 9:7 Matthew 5:3 2 Corinthians 8:9.

MAY YOUR KINDNESS, O LORD

"May your kindness, O Lord, be upon us
who have put our hope in you."

To those who have little hope,
    you give little.

To those who have much hope,
    you give much.

To us who dare to hope for everything,
give, O Lord, all your love,
you who have offered us everything
    in your Son Jesus Christ.

And if our hearts are too small
to receive your royal generosity,
let your merciful hand, we pray,
    open them to your love.

YOUR PATHS ARE LOVE AND TRUTH

God our Father,
your Holy Spirit moves us to pray in the psalm:
"All of God's paths are love and truth."

Help us to understand, O Lord,
that these words are true!

This joy that overwhelms us,
this grief that consumes us,
this despair that lies in wait for us
    like a savage beast at the bend
    in a path through undergrowth,
and even this dull day,
which covers us like a mantle of boredom,
all these are the way by which
    your love and fidelity come to us.

Psalm 33:22 Romans 8:32 Psalm 25:10.

"I AM GOING TO PREPARE A PLACE FOR YOU"

That empty place in heaven
that you have prepared for me —
remember it always, Lord!

O do not forget me, my God and my love!
See how I labor on the way!

Send me your holy angels
that I may not get lost on the road!

And all my friends who are already at home with you,
quickly let them run to meet me
    that I may not be late
for the eternal celebration of your mercy!

GOD OUR FATHER

God our Father,
you who are Love,
you who give to this Love
the face of a man in your Son Jesus Christ,
    we pray:

Help us never to doubt your tenderness,
to entrust ourselves always to your mercy,
and to walk humbly with your Son,
our Lord and our brother.
    Amen.

John 14:2   John 3:16   1 John 4:8, 16.

CARRY THE CROSS EACH DAY

Lord Jesus, you know how earnestly we wish
"instant" joy and happiness, right now,
    without waiting a moment longer.
Yet you tell us:
"Whoever wish to be my followers,
must deny their very selves,
take up their crosses each day,
and follow in my steps."

Grant that we may never be ashamed of these words
    in the presence of our brothers and sisters,
but rather accept them as a rule of life.
For to follow you is to find the cross;
but your cross is a source of joy,
and your joy, during this very day, is the gate to eternity!

FATHER, SOURCE OF ALL JOY

God our Father,
source of all joy in heaven as on earth,
prepare for all people, we pray,
    the banquet of eternal joy.

Remove the mourning veil covering all peoples
and the shroud investing all nations.

Destroy death forever
in the resurrection of your Son Jesus.

Wipe away the tears from every cheek;
take away the shame of the people who love you.

    Because you are God
for the joy and gladness of all people,
you have not created death or invented tears;
but you call all people to be brothers and sisters of Jesus,
to share your life and joy
    forever.

Luke 9:23-26 Isaiah 25:6-8 Wisdom 1:13 1 Corinthians 15:26.

YES, FATHER, FOR THAT IS YOUR GRACIOUS WILL

We thank you, God our Father,
for having taught us to say with your Spirit
    who dwells in our hearts:
"Yes, Father, for that is your gracious will!"

When we say this "yes"
in our joys as well as in our sorrows,
    be so kind as to recognize
the voice of Jesus, your beloved Son!

THE WIDOW OF NAIM

May you be blessed, Lord Jesus,
for the day when you encountered the tears
    of the widow of Naim!

God unchangeable in your eternity,
infinite in your goodness,
you whom no misery of ours can affect,
to whose joy no one can add,
    or from which no one can subtract:
May you be blessed, because in Jesus Christ
you allowed yourself to be moved by the tears
    of a widow.

May you be blessed, because now we know
    the God eternal
    has a human heart.
Let our misery become your misery,
so that your joy may become our joy.

Matthew 11:26   Luke 10:21   Luke 7:11-17.

TWO BROTHERS

For a very long time,
two brothers have been at war with each other
and have made the heart of their father sad.

One is the Jewish people, born of Isaac;
the other, the Arabs, born of Ishmael.
Both are sons of Abraham.

You also, Lord Jesus,
are a son of Abraham.

You who, by your cross, have destroyed hatred
and established the peace of God,
reconcile your brothers according to the flesh,
so that the people born of Abraham
may finally be the people of peace.

And, at the time foreseen according to your mercy,
let them recognize you
for their Savior and their brother.

THE AMEN OF OUR LOVE

Praise and glory to you, Jesus,
our Lord and our brother!

In you "Yes" and "No" were never found
    side by side;
rather for our sakes you were the total "Yes,"
which the love of God pronounced on our behalf,
and in which he kept all his promises.

    We pray to you:
Please be our "Amen" of love that we offer
    in return
      for the love of your Father.

The Amen of Our Love, *2 Corinthians 1:20-22.*

MORNING

PRAYERS

GIVE US, O LORD

Let us ask the Father of lights,
from whom we receive every gift,
to open our hearts to his grace:
  Lord, grant us your love.

Give us, O Lord,
a day filled with your presence
and bright with your love.
    Lord, grant us your love.

Give us, O Lord,
your angel to guide us on our way
and to watch over our souls and bodies.
    Lord, grant us your love.

Give us, O Lord,
your joy in our sadness,
your light in our darkness.
    Lord, grant us your love.

Give us, O Lord,
our daily bread,
and forgive us our sins.
    Lord, grant us your love.

Give us, O Lord,
a life lived in grace,
a death in the peace of your love.
    Lord, grant us your love.

Give us, O Lord,
your mercy on the last day,
and the Kingdom you have prepared for us.
    Lord, grant us your love.

PRAYER OF CONTEMPLATION

In the morning,
I sing your praise, O Lord.

Lord, you have always given me
    tomorrow's bread,
and, although I am poor,
    today I believe.

Lord, you have always mapped out
    tomorrow's road,
and, although it is hidden,
    today I believe.

Lord, you have always given me
    tomorrow's peace,
and, in spite of my distress,
    today I believe.

Lord, you have always given me
    tomorrow's strength,
and, although I am weak,
    today I believe.

Lord, you have always given me
    tomorrow's light,
and, in spite of the darkness,
    today I believe.

Lord, you have always spoken
    when I was in doubt,
and, in spite of your silence,
    today I believe.

Lord, you are my life;
    you are my endless joy.
Even in death
    forever I believe.

PRAYER OF PSALM 146

(In the morning, Ps 90:14)

Fill us with your love in the morning
and we will live the whole day
in joy and praise.
> *Lord, listen to us.*

(In the evening, Ps 141:2)

Let my prayer rise before you like incense,
and my hands like the evening offering.
> *Lord, listen to us.*

Restore sight to the blind;
straighten those who are bent.
> Lord, listen to us.

Protect the weak and the needy;
support the widow and the orphan.
> Lord, listen to us.

Come and cure all broken hearts;
give justice to the oppressed.
> Lord, listen to us.

Give bread to the hungry;
give freedom to prisoners.
> Lord, listen to us.

May your eternal Kingdom be ours;
give salvation to those who love you.
> Lord, listen to us.

IF TODAY YOU HEAR HIS VOICE

God of truth, you who said to us,
"If today you hear my voice,
harden not your hearts,"
we pray to you at the beginning of this day.

You who speak to us through the marvels of creation,
which you give us for our joy:
Open our eyes that we may recognize therein
the trace of your steps.

You who speak to us through today's happenings:
Make us attentive so as to discern your holy will
in each of our joys and our pains.

You who speak to us through our brothers and sisters:
Help us to discover your face
in the faces of those who surround us.

You who speak to us through your Son, your living Word,
announced by the prophets
and proclaimed by the Evangelists:

You who speak to us even in your silences:

Give us the grace to open our hearts to your calls,
to listen to them with joy,
to follow them with love,
until the twilight of our lives,
when we will arrive at that eternal today,
when we will see you face to face,
forever and ever.
    Amen!

Psalm 95:7-8.

WAKE OUR SLEEPING HEARTS

Our Father in heaven,
you who lead us from the darkness of night
to the brightness of this new day,
    listen to our prayer.

Let your grace wake our sleeping hearts.

Let our words, our thoughts, and our actions,
today and all the days of our lives,
be always concerned with the accomplishment
    of your holy will.

Preserve us from the sadness of sin;
keep us in the joy of your light.

Then, when evening comes,
we will be able, now and always,
to praise, bless, and glorify you,

through Jesus Christ, your beloved Son,
in the unity of the Holy Spirit,
forever and ever.
    Amen!

MAKE YOUR LIGHT SHINE

God our Father, you who said,
"Let there be light shining out of darkness!"
make your light shine in our hearts
so that the knowledge of the glory of God,
which is on the face of Christ,
may shine brightly there.

Throughout this day,
may your mercy be our defense;
your praise, our gladness;
your Word, the treasure of our hearts.

Let your blessing descend on each of our actions.
Let it accompany us and help us reach
the great morning that knows no night,
when we will praise your love unceasingly,

through your Son, Jesus Christ, our Savior and our brother,
in the unity of the love of the Holy Spirit,
forever and ever.
    Amen!

2 Corinthians 4:6.

TO ASSEMBLE FOR YOUR PRAISE

God our Father, you who, in Jesus Christ,
have called us from darkness into your marvelous light
so that we may announce your praises and your splendor:

We bless you; we adore you;
we glorify you at all times,
but especially on this morning
when you have awakened us to assemble for your praise.

Help us today and every day to love you more
by loving our brothers and sisters with greater sincerity.

When the morning of eternal Day dawns,
grant us a place on your right hand.
Then, with smiles on our lips and joy in our hearts,
we will celebrate the strength of your love,
forever and ever.
       Amen!

OPEN MY EAR

Every morning, Lord,
open my ear
that I may hear your Word.

I am your disciple:
Teach me
in your Son Jesus Christ.

1 Peter 2:9 Isaiah 50:4.

THAT WE MAY LEARN TO LOVE YOU

Blessed are you Lord, our Father,
you who give us this new day
to learn to love you more.

Help us today and every day
to look for you and to find you
in the service of our brothers and sisters.

Illumine the eyes of our hearts
so that, in each of our joys and our sorrows,
we will know how to recognize your presence,
to discover your tenderness,
and to live in your peace.

And just as you lead us
from the shades of night to the brightness of morn,
lead us beyond the darkness and joys of this world
to the light and the joy of the eternal Day.

Yours be our love and our praise,
in the Church and Christ Jesus,
forever and ever.
      Amen!

O RISING SUN!

At the dawning of this new day,
Lord Jesus, we offer you our prayer:

Light of life that shines in the darkness!
Be so kind as to bestow on all people,
     our brothers and sisters,
your splendor and your truth
so that they may recognize you as Savior,
and give them your life and your joy
so that they will love you as God.

Gather up into your Kingdom of light
all who have died during the night —
we commend them to your mercy.

Also console with your divine peace
all who, during the night,
have carried the burden of sickness,
the distress of sadness,
or the bitterness of loneliness.

O Rising Sun! Come to light up
those who still sleep in the darkness of death.

Guide our footsteps on the road of peace
to your Father, who is also our Father,
for you are our way, our truth, and our life,
     forever and ever.
     Amen!

Luke 2:78-79   John 8:12; 14:6.

SHOW US THE LIGHT OF YOUR FACE

When daylight comes,
Lord, we give you thanks,
and we implore you:
Show us the light of your face.

Direct and sanctify, rule and govern
our hearts and our bodies,
our feelings, our words and our deeds,
according to your law of love.

Help us today and every day
to share in building a more beautiful world,
founded on Jesus Christ, in justice and love.

By spreading your joy and peace around us,
by driving back the frontiers of suffering and death,
may we be able to announce by our entire lives
the future Kingdom, where you will dry all tears
  on the Day of eternity.
  Amen!

THE SMILE OF YOUR FACE

Lord, the smile of the dawn
lights up the sky.

May the smile of your face
light up our day!

Psalm 4:7.

MAKE YOUR LOVE RISE ON ALL

God of tenderness and pity,
we pray at the beginning of this day:

Just as you cause your sun to rise
on the good and the wicked,
let your love rise on all people, our brothers and sisters.

All that we are, all that we have,
we put back in your hands
so that this day may be completely consecrated.

We offer all to you through Jesus, your beloved Son,
our Lord and our High Priest,
who sits at your right hand
to intercede without ceasing on our behalf
and to help us to enter the eternal Kingdom,
where we will enjoy the fullness of joy and peace,
forever and ever.
       Amen!

Matthew 5:45   Hebrews 7:25.

EVENING
PRAYERS

STAY WITH US, LORD

Stay with us, Lord Jesus Christ!

Stay with us, Lord:
Behold, evening is coming,
and we still have not recognized your face
in each of our brothers and sisters.
Stay with us, Lord Jesus Christ!

Stay with us, Lord:
Behold, evening is coming,
and we still have not shared your bread
in thanksgiving with all our brothers and sisters.
Stay with us, Lord Jesus Christ!

Stay with us, Lord:
Behold, evening is coming,
and we still have not recognized your Word
in the words of all our brothers and sisters.
Stay with us, Lord Jesus Christ!

Stay with us, Lord:
Behold, evening is coming,
and our hearts are still too slow to believe
that you had to die in order to rise again.
Stay with us, Lord Jesus Christ!

Stay with us, Lord,
for our night itself becomes day
     when you are there!
Stay with us, Lord Jesus Christ!

ALL DAY LONG, LORD

Remember us, O Lord,
in your loving care!

All day long, Lord,
I have waited for you on my doorstep,
and, behold, you were in my house!
    Remember us, O Lord,
    in your loving care!

All day long, Lord,
I have looked for you far off in the crowd,
and, behold, you were right next to me,
present in my brother and my sister!
    Remember us, O Lord,
    in your loving care!

All day long, Lord,
my hands remained closed
to protect my happiness,
and, behold, my happiness
was to open them for you!
    Remember us, O Lord,
    in your loving care!

All day long, Lord,
I looked for your Word
in the wisdom of men and women,
and, behold, it was present
in the depths of my heart!
    Remember us, O Lord,
    in your loving care!

I TRUST IN YOU, LORD

Into your hands, O Lord,
I commend my spirit.

I trust in you, Lord; deliver me;
    my life is in your hands;
through your love save me.
Into your hands, O Lord, I commend my spirit.

Look at me; answer me, Lord my God;
    open my eyes
that I may not sleep in death.
Into your hands, O Lord, I commend my spirit.

Guard me like the pupil of your eye;
    hide me
in the shadow of your wings.
Into your hands, O Lord, I commend my spirit.

I lie down and sleep in peace;
    you alone, Lord,
keep me safe.
Into your hands, O Lord, I commend my spirit.

In joy I will look upon your face, Lord;
    when I awake
I will be satisfied with your face.
Into your hands, O Lord, I commend my spirit.

Psalms 4:9; 13:4; 17:8, 15; 31:6, 15-17.

I STAND KNOCKING

Lord Jesus, you who said,
"Here I stand, knocking at the door.
If anyone hears me calling and opens the door,
I will enter his house and have supper with him,
and he with me,"
look at your family gathered together before you.

We have heard your living Word;
we open the door of our community to you;
we pray you be our guest.

Let each one of us
in the joys and sorrows of our way
feel the comfort of your presence.

Beyond the darkness of this world,
lead us to the morning of the eternal Day
when you yourself will invite us
to the banquet of the Kingdom
that your Father prepares for us,
forever and ever.
        Amen!

Revelation 3:20.

COME TO ME, ALL YOU WEARY

Lord Jesus, you who said,
"Come to me, all you who are weary
and find life burdensome,
and I will refresh you,"
    we pray to you:

See our hands tired
    from having searched for vanity.
See our spirits wounded
    from having welcomed pride.
See our hearts now aching
    from having loved all except you.

Help us to understand
that carrying your yoke means to rest,
and refusing your burden means to become tired,
for your yoke is easy and your burden light.

Just as you give us this night
    to rest our bodies,
give us your tenderness
    to rest our souls.

By a life rich in good works
    toward our brothers and sisters,
lead us to the kingdom of eternal rest,
where we will experience the fullness of joy and peace
close to our Father, in the love of the Spirit,

forever and ever.
    Amen!

Matthew 11:28-29.

THE EYES OF MARY

Lord Jesus,
have pity on me!

With Martha,
I was busy all day long.

Allow me now,
with Mary,
to sit at your feet
simply to look at you.

THE TIRED HANDS OF MARTHA

Lord Jesus,
I would have chosen, like Mary,
to sit all day long in peace
    at your feet
and listen to the silence of my heart.

But you came into my house
with all your friends
who kept me busy,
and I served them for love of you.

If I cannot offer you
the eyes of Mary,
accept at least, I pray you,
the tired hands of Martha.
They are my love for you.

Luke 10:38-42.

BEYOND THE NIGHT

When evening comes,
Lord, we pray:

We thank you for this day
filled with your presence.

We praise and bless you
for the joy of those who love one another,
for the efforts of those who work,
for the patience of those who suffer,
for every good work that people
have accomplished in your honor today.

We ask pardon of you
for the weakness of our love
on the road that leads to you.

Lead us beyond the night
to the dawn of the eternal Day
when we will see you face to face.

You who are our Father,
your Son Jesus Christ,
who is our Savior and our brother,
and the Holy Spirit who dwells in our hearts,

forever and ever.
    Amen!

LORD JESUS, COME AMONG US

Lord Jesus, who came among us
to call not the virtuous, but the sinners,
it is to you we pray:

With confidence we present ourselves before you,
in spite of our weakness, because you forgive us
not because of our deeds
but according to the abundance of your love.

Gather together your Church,
torn apart by our sins and divisions.
Gather together also our hearts,
scattered by the vanities of this world.

Grant us finally a peaceful evening,
a night of quiet rest,
a morning filled with joy and zeal to serve you.

You are the hope of our lives and our Savior,
forever and ever.
     Amen!

Matthew 9:13.

VISIT OUR COMMUNITY

We ask you, Lord:
Visit our community,
which your love put together.

Remove far from it
every attack of the enemy.

Let your holy angels dwell with us
to keep us in peace.

Let your blessing and your love
come to rest on each one of us.

Save us through your Son Jesus Christ,
who died and rose again for us,
so that, awake or asleep,
we may always live in the joy of your presence,

forever and ever.
   Amen!

THE CUP OF OUR DAY

When evening comes,
we present to you, Lord,
the cup of our day.

It is empty, you know —
fill it with your pardon.

And our hearts will rest then
in peace and joy.

1 Thessalonians 5:9-10.

WHEN CHRIST, THE MORNING STAR, RISES

We bless you, O God, our Father,
through your only Son, Jesus Christ, the Lord.

Having ended this day,
having arrived at the borders of night,
having been satisfied by the light of the day
that you created for our joy, we thank you
and ask for your kindness.

Just as you hide all things
in the darkness of night,
please cover our faults
in your endless mercy.

Be so kind as to send your holy angels
to keep us in peace
and protect us on the roads of our lives.

Gather us into the Kingdom of eternal light
on the day when Christ, the Morning Star,
rises in our hearts.

We ask this of you through Jesus Christ,
your Son, our Lord,
who lives and reigns with you in the unity
of the Holy Spirit,
God forever and ever.
Amen!

2 Peter 1:19.

YOURS ARE THE TIMES OF OUR LIVES

When evening comes,
Lord, we thank you.

Yours is the day; yours is the night;
yours also are the times of our lives:
They are in your hand;
we entrust them to your mercy.

Let the end of this day,
which increases the number of days in our lives,
increase also our love for you.

Forgive us our weaknesses,
you who find joy in showing mercy.

Let nothing hinder us on our way to you.
By our holy lives and our prayers
may we be able to hasten the coming of that day
when you will open the gate of your mercy
to those seeking your love.

To you be glory and power,
through Jesus Christ, your beloved Son,
in the unity of the Holy Spirit,
now and until the day of eternity.
    Amen!

Psalm 74:16   Micah 7:18   2 Peter 3:11-12.

THE BRIDEGROOM IS HERE

Lord Jesus,
see your community assembled before you
for your praise in the evening.

We return to you this day
that your goodness has given us.
Let its joy as well as its dullness
reveal your love to us.

Forgive our weaknesses,
you who are the fullness of mercy.
Take away our fatigue,
you who are the repose of our souls.

Help us to stay awake
and wait joyfully for your return.

When you do return in the middle of the night,
let us be ready to run to you.
When the cry resounds
"The bridegroom is here!"
let us go in with you to the banquet of your Kingdom,

where you reign with your Father,
who is also our Father,
in union with the Spirit of love,
forever and ever.
        Amen!

Matthew 25:6.

A SOURCE OF LIVING WATER

This day has passed away
like water that runs through our fingers.

Lord, we thirst for eternity.
Unearth in our hearts a source of living water
that springs forth unto eternal life.

JOY AND BEAUTY

Lord Jesus, the joy and beauty
of every moment of my life!

Be the last melody of my day song
as it fades into the night.

And tomorrow,
when my eyes greet the morning,
be my first ray of sunlight.

WE BLESS YOU

We bless you, Lord Jesus,
Light born of the Light.

Teach us to flee the darkness of this world
and to hasten toward the day
that the sadness of night
cannot darken.

John 4:14.

GIVE TO MY EYES

Blest be you, Lord Jesus!

Give to my eyes a light sleep
so that my voice, to praise you,
does not remain silent too long.

Your creation will stay awake
so that it may sing with the angels.
May my sleep, in your presence,
be a prayer arising to you.

Let the night retain no faults
    of the past day.
Let not the madness of the night
    invade my dreams.
Even in sleep let my spirit, Lord,
    sing to you.

God, Father and Son and Holy Spirit,
to you be honor, power, and glory,
forever and ever.

St. Gregory Nazianzen (+ 390).

BLESSINGS

Blessed be you, Lord, God of tenderness and compassion,
    rich in kindness and faithfulness,
who keep us in your love forever!   —*Amen.*

The Lord our God is a God of mercy.
To him be glory forever!   —*Amen.*

May the Lord bless us and keep us!   —*Amen.*
May the Lord let his face shine on us
    and be gracious to us!   —*Amen.*
May the Lord show his face to us
    and give us his peace!   —*Amen.*

Blessed be our God from everlasting to everlasting!   —*Amen.*
    And blessed be your name of glory,
which surpasses all blessing and praise!   —*Amen.*

Blessed be God!   —*Amen.*
Blessed be his great name!   —*Amen.*
Blessed be all his holy angels!   —*Amen.*
Blessed be his great name forevermore!   —*Amen.*
Blessed be all his angels forever!   —*Amen.*

Blessed be the Lord, the God of Israel,
    who alone performs marvels!   —*Amen.*
Blessed forever be his glorious name!   —*Amen.*
May the whole world be filled with his glory!   —*Amen.*

    Blessed be you, Lord,
God of the humble and help of the oppressed!   —*Amen.*
    Blessed be you, Lord,
support of the weak and refuge of the forsaken!   —*Amen.*
    Blessed be you, Lord,
savior of the despairing — to you be eternal glory!   —*Amen.*

Blessed be you, Father, Lord of heaven and earth!   —*Amen.*
You hide your mystery from the learned and clever,
but you reveal it to mere children.   —*Amen.*
Yes, Father, for such is your gracious will.   —*Amen.*

Exodus 34:6-7   Deuteronomy 4:31   Numbers 6:24-26   Nehemiah 9:5
Tobias 11:4   Psalm 72:18-19   Judith 9:11   Matthew 11:25-26.

May you be blessed, Lord Jesus,
who died for our sins
and rose again for our life!   — *Amen.*
To you be glory forever!   — *Amen.*

Blessed be the God of hope and consolation!   — *Amen.*
May he help us all to be tolerant with one another,
following the example of Jesus Christ!   — *Amen.*
So that, united in mind and voice, we may give glory
to the God and Father of our Lord Jesus Christ!   — *Amen.*

May the God of hope fill us
with every joy and with peace, in the faith!   — *Amen.*
May hope overflow in us
    through the power of the Holy Spirit!   — *Amen.*

To the Father, who can give us the strength to live
according to the Gospel and the message of Jesus Christ,
to him, the God who alone is wise, through Jesus Christ,
be glory and power forever!   — *Amen.*
May God our Father strengthen us until the last day
    so that we may be without blame
    on the Day of our Lord Jesus Christ!   — *Amen.*
He is faithful, he who calls us
to fellowship with his Son Jesus, our Lord.   — *Amen.*
    To him be glory forever!   — *Amen.*

Let us give thanks to God, who gives us victory
    through our Lord Jesus Christ!   — *Amen.*

Marana tha! Come, Lord Jesus!   — *Amen.*
Your grace be with us all!   — *Amen.*

Blessed be the God and Father
of our Lord Jesus Christ,
a gentle Father and the God of all consolation
who comforts us in all our sorrows!   — *Amen.*

Blessed be God our Father,
who raised his Son Jesus Christ to life!   — *Amen.*
He will raise us one day with him
and place us together by his side.   — *Amen.*

Romans 4:25; 15:5-6; 16:25, 27   1 Corinthians 1:8-9; 15:57; 16:23-24
2 Corinthians 1:3-4; 4:14.

The grace of our Lord Jesus Christ,
the love of God the Father,
and the fellowship of the Holy Spirit
    be with us all!   *— Amen.*

The grace and peace of God our Father
    and the Lord Jesus Christ!   *— Amen.*
He sacrificed himself for our sins
to rescue us from this present wicked world
    in accordance with the will of his Father.   *— Amen.*
To him be glory forever!   *— Amen.*

Blessed be the God and Father
    of our Lord Jesus Christ,
who has filled us with blessings in Christ!   *— Amen.*

Glory to God our Father,
from generation to generation,
in the Church and in Christ Jesus!   *— Amen.*

May God the Father and the Lord Jesus
grant peace, love, and faith to all our brothers and sisters! *— Amen.*
May grace be with all who love
    our Lord Jesus Christ!   *— Amen.*

    May God our Father,
who has begun an excellent work in us,
    see that it is finished
when the Day of Christ Jesus comes!   *— Amen.*
To him be glory forever!   *— Amen.*

May the peace of God that is beyond all understanding
guard our hearts and our thoughts in Christ Jesus!   *— Amen.*

May God our Father fulfill all our needs
according to his generosity, with magnificence,
    in Christ Jesus!   *— Amen.*
To him be glory forever!   *— Amen.*

We give you thanks, our Father!   *— Amen.*
You call us to share the lot of the saints
    in light!   *— Amen.*

2 Corinthians 13:13   Galatians 1:3-5   Ephesians 1:3-4; 3:21; 6:23-24
Philippians 1:6; 4:7; 4:19-20   Colossians 1:12.

You rescue us from the power of darkness
and bring us into the Kingdom
    of your beloved Son.   *— Amen.*

May the peace of God reign in our hearts,
that peace to which we are called together
    as parts of one Body.   *— Amen.*
In all our words and actions
let us give thanks to God our Father,
    in the name of the Lord Jesus.   *— Amen.*

May God our Father put our faith into action,
to work for love, to preserve hope,
    through our Lord Jesus Christ.   *— Amen.*

May the Lord help us to grow and abound
    in love for one another.   *— Amen.*
May he confirm our hearts in holiness without blame
    before God our Father,
at the time of his coming with all his saints.   *— Amen.*

    Blessed be God our Father,
who gives salvation through our Lord Jesus Christ.   *— Amen.*
    He died and rose again for us
    so that, awake or asleep,
we might live together with him.   *— Amen.*

    May the Lord of peace himself
give us peace all the time
    and in every way!   *— Amen.*
The Lord be with us all!   *— Amen.*

Grace, mercy, and peace from God our Father
    and Christ Jesus, our Lord!   *— Amen.*

    To the eternal King,
the immortal, invisible, and only God,
be honor and glory forever and ever!   *— Amen.*

To the blessed and only ruler of all,
to the King of kings and Lord of lords,
who alone is immortal,
whose home is unapproachable light,

Colossians 1:13; 3:15-17 1 Thessalonians 1:2; 3:12-13; 5:9-10
2 Thessalonians 3:16 1 Timothy 1:2; 1:17; 6:15.

whom no man has ever seen or can see,
to him be honor and everlasting power! — *Amen.*

    Jesus Christ, the same
yesterday, today, and forever. — *Amen.*
To him be glory forever! — *Amen.*

May God be glorified in all things through Jesus Christ! — *Amen.*
To him be glory and power forever and ever! — *Amen.*

May the God of all grace who has called us
to his everlasting glory in Christ Jesus,
    after brief suffering,
restore us to himself and confirm us. — *Amen.*
May he strengthen us and make us steadfast. — *Amen.*
To him be power forever and ever! — *Amen.*

May grace and peace be given us in abundance
    as we come to know God
        and Jesus, our Lord! — *Amen.*
To him be glory forever and ever! — *Amen.*

May we grow in the grace and knowledge
of our Lord and Savior, Jesus Christ! — *Amen.*
To him be glory now and in eternity! — *Amen.*

To him who can keep you from falling
and bring you safely into his glorious presence,
innocent and happy,
to the only God, our Savior, through Jesus our Lord,
be glory, majesty, authority, and power,
from even before the beginning of time,
through the present,
and for all ages to come. — *Amen.*

Praise, glory, and wisdom,
thanksgiving, honor, power, and strength,
    to our God
        forever and ever! — *Amen.*

Amen! Come, Lord Jesus! — *Amen.*
May your grace be with us all! — *Amen.*

*1 Timothy 6:16 Hebrews 13:8 1 Peter 4:11; 5:10-11 2 Peter 1:2; 3:18
Jude 24-25 Revelation 7:12; 22:21.*

RESPONSES

FOR THE

LITANIES

1. Al - le - lu - ia,— Al - le - lu - ia, Al - le - lu - ia!

2. Blest are those who are in - vit - ed— to the ban - quet of the King - dom!

3. Blest are you, O Lord, through e - ter - ni - ty!

4. (A) Come, Lord Je - sus, come!
   or
   (B) Come, Lord Je - sus Christ.

5. Come, O Lord, come, save your peo - ple!

6. Come to pray in us, Spir - it of the Lord!

7. Come to us, Spir - it of the Lord!

8. De - liv - er us, O Lord!

9. Em - man - u - el! Come, save your peo - ple!

10. Glo - ry and praise to you, Lord Je - sus Christ!

11. Glo - ry to God on high!

12. Grant to us your love.

13. Grant to us your sal - va - tion.

14. Have mer - cy, O Lord, have mer - cy on us!

15. Have mer - cy, O Lord, have mer - cy on us!

16. Hear us, Lord, show us mer - cy!

17. Help us to fast, O Lord, by lov-ing one an - oth - er.

18. Ho-ly, ho-ly, ho-ly is the Lord,— for e -ter-nal is his love!

19. In the morn-ing, I sing your praise, O Lord.

20. In - to your hands, O Lord, I com -mend my spir - it.

21. Je - sus Christ, ris - en Lord, have mer - cy on us!

22. Joy to you, O Vir-gin Mar -y, Moth-er of the Lord!

23. Lead us not in - to temp - ta - tion,

but de - liv - er us from e - vil!

306

24 Let the light of your face shine up-on us!

25 Lord, have mer - cy.

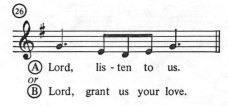

26 A Lord, lis-ten to us.
or
B Lord, grant us your love.

27 Ma - ra - na tha! Come, Lord Je - sus, come!

28 May you be blest, O Lord!

29 My Lord and my God!

30 O God, be mer-ci-ful to me, a sin-ner!

31. O Lord, we pray to you.

32. O - pen my eyes, O Je - sus, Lord.

33. Praise to you, Lord Je - sus Christ, King of end - less glo - ry!

34. Praise to you now and ev - er - more!

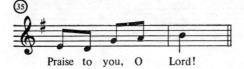

35. Praise to you, O Lord!

36. Pray to the Lord for us.

37. Re - mem - ber us, O Lord, in your King - dom.

38. Re - mem - ber us, O Lord, in your lov - ing care.

39 Save us, O Lord, grant to us your love.

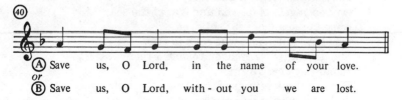

40 (A) Save us, O Lord, in the name of your love.

or

(B) Save us, O Lord, with - out you we are lost.

41 Show to us your mer - cy, Lord our God.

42 Stay with us, Lord Je - sus Christ!

43 Those trust-ing in you, O Lord, will nev- er be de - ceived.

44 We sing your praise, O Lord.

45 You are my love, O Lord, you are my joy!

46 Your king - dom come, O Lord!

HOLY MOTHER

Holy Mother of our Redeemer,
ever open gate of heaven and star of the sea,
come to the aid of your children
who have fallen and who seek to rise.
You gave birth, O Wonder, to your Creator,
remaining ever virgin.
Receive the greetings of the Angel Gabriel,
and have pity on us sinners.

HAIL, HOLY QUEEN

Hail, holy Queen of the Heavens!
Hail, holy Queen of the Angels!
Hail, Root of Jesse!
Hail, Gate of Heaven!
By you the Light has entered the world.
Rejoice, glorious Virgin,
beautiful among all women.
Hail, radiant Splendor,
intercede with Christ for us.

QUEEN OF HEAVEN

Queen of Heaven, rejoice, Alleluia!
For the Lord whom you were worthy to bear, Alleluia!
Has risen as he said, Alleluia!
Pray for us to God, Alleluia!

WE PLACE OURSELVES

We place ourselves in your keeping,
    holy Mother of God.
Do not refuse the prayer of your children
    in their distress.
But deliver us from all danger,
Ever Virgin, glorious and blessed!

For the musical settings of these texts, see Deiss, *Biblical Hymns and Psalms*, Vol. I.

LITURGICAL USE OF THE PSALTER
according to the *Lectionary*

Liturgical Cycle

Advent: 25, 85 and also 24, 89, 122, 126, 146.

Christmas: 96, 98 and also 40.

Holy Family: 128.

Epiphany: 72.

Lent: 25, 51, 91, 130 and also 19, 23, 27, 32, 34, 103, 126, 137, 139.

Passion: 22, 69 and also 40.

Easter: 118, 136 and also 4, 16, 23, 27, 33, 68, 98, 100, 103, 139, 145, 150.

Ascension: 47, 68.

Pentecost: 104.

Trinity: 8, 33 and Canticle of Daniel (p. 87).

Corpus Christi: 117, 147. See also *Eucharist.*

Sacred Heart: 103 and also 23, 25, 33, 34, 103.

Christ the King: 23, 24, 122.

Virgin Mary: 113, 122, 127, 147, Magnificat (p. 112).

Other Circumstances

Angels: 138 and also 91.

Baptism: 42 and also 8, 23, 27, 32, 33, 51, 65, 126.

Church: 84, 95, 100, 121, 149, and Prayer of David (p. 85).

Confirmation: 23, 89, 96, 104, 117, 145.

Death: 23, 25, 27, 31, 42, 103, 117, 122, 130.

Eucharist: 23, 34, 110, 116, 117, 145.

Evening: 4, 16, 91, 134, Magnificat (p. 112), Canticle of Simeon (p. 112).

Family and Marriage: 128 and also 33, 34, 103, 112, 148.

Harvest: 65, 67.

Holy Cross: 22, 118.

Holy Name of Jesus: 8, 112.

Holy Spirit: 23, 96, 104, 117, 145.

Hunger: 112, 146.

Labor: 127.

Mission: 86, 96, 98, 117.

Morning: 5, 57, 63, Canticle of Zechariah (p. 113).

Old Age: 71, 92.

Peace: 72, 85, 122.

Penitence: 51, 103, 130.

Pilgrimage: Song of Ascents, 121, 122, 123, 126, 127, 128, 130, 131.

Sickness: 103, 116, 146.

Thanksgiving: 103, 111, 113, 116, 138, 145, 149, 150.

Unity: 23, 100, 118, 122, 147.

promise, of the Father, 4
Promised Land, the, 73, 144

reconciliation, through Jesus Christ, 45
redeemer, the Lord as, 2, 54, 71, 92, 101, 119
redemption, through Jesus, 176
refuge, in the Lord, 12, 21, 40, 48, 64
resurrection of Jesus Christ, 2, 9, 11-12, 63, 65, 69, 110, 158, 162-169, 172, 174-175, 184, 203, 211, 214, 230, 267, 299
resurrection of Lazarus, 155
resurrection through Jesus Christ, 4, 9, 102, 144, 155, 164-165, 174, 218
return of Jesus Christ, 121, 124-126
revelation, light of, 40
rock, the Lord as, 21, 28, 40
ruler, the Lord as, 30, 35, 47, 51-52, 133
Ruth, 97

sacrifice of Jesus Christ, 2, 158
salvation: through faith, 109; through the Lord, 2, 52, 112, 119
salvation through Jesus Christ, 9, 71, 122, 141, 151, 158, 175, 190, 204, 206-207, 212, 215, 228, 249, 292, 301
Samuel, 96
Sanhedrin, 182
Savior, Jesus Christ as, 2, 9, 11, 20, 23, 27, 53, 59, 63, 74, 118, 120, 127, 131, 152-153, 280, 290-291, 302. *See also* Lord as Savior
Savior, the Lord as, 18, 27, 36, 62, 64-65, 89, 102, 105-106, 112, 302. *See also* Jesus Christ as Savior
Sermon on the Mount, xiv
sheep: of the Lord, 3, 50, 53, 258; lost, 145, 154
shepherd, Jesus Christ as, 158, 170, 175, 239, 258. *See also* Jesus Christ as Good Shepherd, Lord as shepherd
shepherd, the Lord as, 3, 16, 119, 245. *See also* Jesus as Good Shepherd, Jesus Christ as shepherd
Simeon, 40, 132, 181, 195, 199; Canticle of, 112; prayer of, 40

Simon of Cyrene, 156
sin, original, 148
sinners, called by Jesus, 145, 154, 291
Sirach, prayer of, 85
Son of Abraham, Jesus as, 195, 237
Son of David, Jesus as, 47, 58, 64, 110, 119, 195, 217, 237
Son of Man, Jesus as, 70, 122, 212, 227, 237
Sower, Parable of the, 223
Spirit, Holy. *See* Holy Spirit
spouse, the Lord as, 103, 295
Stephen, 166
stronghold, the Lord as, 40, 48

tax collector, prayer of the, 31, 106
temple, the, 37, 48, 58, 81; cleansing of, 38; presentation of Jesus in, 199
temple of the Lord, 10, 19, 51, 75. *See also* house of the Lord
temptation of Jesus, 48, 149-150, 181, 219
Thomas, 167
throne of the Lord, 10, 30, 61, 101, 114, 226, 253
transfiguration of Jesus, 150, 214
True Vine, Jesus as, 210, 231, 239
trust, in the Lord, 9, 14, 26, 101, 120-121, 286

unity: in the Church, 186; in faith, 36, 234; in Jesus Christ, 109, 169; in the Lord, 4, 107

Visitation, the, 198

water, of eternal life, 28, 296
way, of the Lord, 46
widow of Naim, 217, 268
Wise Men, 132, 139-140, 195, 211
Word, the, 13, 34, 69, 81, 94, 133, 149, 171, 200, 206, 209-210, 213, 223, 246, 251, 261, 277-278, 284-285, 287; Jesus as, 13, 138, 195, 237-239, 275; life-giving, 4; living, 110
works of the Lord, 56-57, 59, 72-73. *See also* Lord as creator

Zachaeus, 145
Zechariah, 181; Canticle of, 113

TITLE INDEX

ADDITIONAL COPYRIGHT NOTICES